# 13 RULES

## FOR BEING AN

# ENTREPRENEUR

Alan Knott-Craig

Dedicated to Mbulelo Ncetezo,
the man who taught me the
importance of respect.

*You don't have to get into a giant laser sword fight
and blow up three spaceships to be a hero.
Help someone. Be compassionate.
Treat others with dignity.*

— GEORGE LUCAS —

*The real hero is always a hero by mistake;*
*he dreams of being an honest coward*
*like everyone else.*

— Umberto Eco —

Do you want to be an entrepreneur?
Do you want to financial freedom?
Good news! Anyone can be an entrepreneur.

You just need to work harder than anyone you know.
And you need to get married young.
And you need to get lucky.

Being an entrepreneur is a heroic endeavour.
You choose to step out into the wilderness.
Into the great unknown.
You choose to take responsibility for your financial future.
You choose to forego the safety of a monthly salary.
You choose a life of uncertainty.
You choose to be an entrepreneur.

The hard part is not wanting to be an entrepreneur.
The hard part is paying the price to be an entrepreneur.

So, the question is:
**Are you willing to pay the price?**

# CONTENTS

1. The Beginning ........................................................ 1
   Follow Your Dreams                                        2
   Don't Follow Your Passion                                 5
   Love Life                                                 6
   Keep Moving                                               7
   Stop Trying to Save the World                             8
   Do Your Best                                             10

2. Values ............................................................. 11
   Be Loyal                                                 12
   Be Respectful                                            12
   Take Responsibility                                      13
   Persevere                                                13
   Do the Right Thing                                       14
   Underpromise                                             15
   Be Humble                                                15

3. Character .......................................................... 17
   Seven Attributes of an Entrepreneur                      18
   Be Equanimous                                            20
   Have a Sense of Humor                                    21
   There Is No Try; There Is Only Do                        24
   Make It Look Easy                                        25
   Go the Extra Mile                                        26
   Give It Your Best Shot! No Excuses                       27
   Help Other People                                        28
   Make Haste Slowly                                        29
   Tell the Truth                                           30
   Never Lie                                                31
   Maximize Your Energy                                     33
   Thirteen Things an Entrepreneur Doesn't Do               34

4. Philosophy ........................................... 35

   Be Antifragile ..................................... 36

   Be Stoic ............................................ 38

   Dealing with Uncertainty ....................... 41

   Don't Be Fooled by Randomness ............... 43

   Thirteen Rules for Happiness .................. 44

   Control Your Destiny ............................. 46

   Listen to the Universe .......................... 47

5. Self-Awareness ..................................... 49

   Know Thyself ...................................... 51

   Know What You Don't Know .................... 52

   Know Your Motives ............................... 52

   Use Your Natural Gifts .......................... 53

   Your Reputation Doesn't Matter ............... 54

   Focus on Your Talents ........................... 55

   Ego Is Like a Dragon ............................ 56

6. Habits ............................................... 57

   Make Your Bed in the Morning ................ 58

   Don't Be too Proud to Do the Dirty Work ... 59

   Write Every Day .................................. 60

   Wake Up Early .................................... 61

   Have Good Manners .............................. 62

   Avoid Small Decisions ........................... 63

   Wash Your Hands ................................. 64

   Live Simply ........................................ 65

   Smile and Wave ................................... 65

   Be a Paranoid Optimist ......................... 66

   Nap ................................................. 67

   Meditate ........................................... 67

   Pray ................................................ 69

7. **People** 71

Find Your Tribe 67

Be Yourself 75

Watch Out for Slackers 76

Beware of People Who Keep Their Options Open 78

Don't Let Friends Hold You Back 79

Don't Let People Upset You 80

Stay Away from Energy Vampires 81

8. **Adversity** 83

Defeat Is Okay 84

Stop Waiting for Someone to Save You 86

Don't Be a Victim 87

Don't Blame Other People 88

Tackle Obstacles Head On 89

Don't Run Away 90

Forget about Revenge 91

Take It on the Chin 92

Four Steps for Recovering from Failure 92

There's Only One Way Out of a Jam 94

Sometimes You Have to Play Dead 94

Seven Tricks for Fighting Fear 95

This Too Shall Pass 96

9. **Learning** 97

Tell Your Story 99

Seven Tips to Improve Your Memory 100

Six Rules for Writing 101

The Difference between Thinkers and Doers 102

Twenty-Three Tips for Becoming a Better Negotiator 103

The Art of Selling 104

Change Your Mind 107

10. **Family** 109

Don't Neglect Your Family . . . . . . . . . . . . . . . . . . . . . . . . . . . . 110
Seven Reasons to Marry Young . . . . . . . . . . . . . . . . . . . . . . . . 111
Seven Ways Children Make You a Better Person . . . . . 113
Make a Living and Live at the Same Time . . . . . . . . . . . . 115
Be Present . . . . . . . . . . . . . . . . . . . . . . . . . . . . . . . . . . . . . . . . . . . . 116
Teach Your Children . . . . . . . . . . . . . . . . . . . . . . . . . . . . . . . . . . 117
The Six-Month Rule . . . . . . . . . . . . . . . . . . . . . . . . . . . . . . . . . . . 118

11. Courage . . . . . . . . . . . . . . . . . . . . . . . . . . . . . . . . . . . . . . . . . . . . . . 119
Go into the Lion's Den . . . . . . . . . . . . . . . . . . . . . . . . . . . . . . . . 120
The Man in the Arena . . . . . . . . . . . . . . . . . . . . . . . . . . . . . . . . . 121
The Courage to Copy Cowards . . . . . . . . . . . . . . . . . . . . . . . 122
The Courage to Follow . . . . . . . . . . . . . . . . . . . . . . . . . . . . . . . 122
The Courage to Fight . . . . . . . . . . . . . . . . . . . . . . . . . . . . . . . . . 122
The Courage to Lead . . . . . . . . . . . . . . . . . . . . . . . . . . . . . . . . . 123
The Courage to Speak Up . . . . . . . . . . . . . . . . . . . . . . . . . . . . 123
The Courage to Carry on . . . . . . . . . . . . . . . . . . . . . . . . . . . . . 123
The Courage to Quit . . . . . . . . . . . . . . . . . . . . . . . . . . . . . . . . . . 124
The Courage to Ignore the Crowd . . . . . . . . . . . . . . . . . . . 125
The Courage to Face the Truth . . . . . . . . . . . . . . . . . . . . . . . 126
The Courage to Face the Fear of Failure . . . . . . . . . . . . . 127
"If," by Rudyard Kipling . . . . . . . . . . . . . . . . . . . . . . . . . . . . . . 128

12. Pearls of Wisdom . . . . . . . . . . . . . . . . . . . . . . . . . . . . . . . . . . . . 129
The Purpose-Driven Life, by Rick Warren . . . . . . . . . . . . 130
Leadership, DPJ style . . . . . . . . . . . . . . . . . . . . . . . . . . . . . . . . . 132
Guarding Your Passion, by Lynette Finlay . . . . . . . . . . . . 134
Words of Wisdom, by Michael Jordaan . . . . . . . . . . . . . . . 134
Lessons Learned in My First Eighty Years
    by Byron Wien . . . . . . . . . . . . . . . . . . . . . . . . . . . . . . . . . . . . . 135
"Excellence," by Lewis Pugh . . . . . . . . . . . . . . . . . . . . . . . . . . 138
Leadership Matters, by Brand Pretorius . . . . . . . . . . . . . . 142

Management Tips, *by Alex Ferguson*     143

True Tales of a Fun, Fearless Female,

    *by Jane Raphaely*     144

"Notes to Self," *by Kim van Kets*     147

How to Achieve Success, *by Yusuf Abramjee*     149

Letter from a Dad     150

Lessons from Winston Churchill     152

Ten Ways to Change the World,

    *by Admiral William McRaven*     154

Dangers to Human Virtue, *by Mahatma Gandhi*     155

"Ten Tips from a Buddhist Monk,"

    *by Charlene Barry*     156

Books to Read     160

13. **The End**     167

Luck Is Real     168

Believe in Yourself     170

The Secret to Achieving Your Dreams     171

About the Author     173

## "The Road Not Taken"

by Robert Frost

*Two roads diverged in a yellow wood,*
*And sorry I could not travel both*
*And be one traveler, long I stood*
*And looked down one as far as I could*
*To where it bent in the undergrowth;*

*Then took the other, as just as fair,*
*And having perhaps the better claim*
*Because it was grassy and wanted wear,*
*Though as for that the passing there*
*Had worn them really about the same,*

*And both that morning equally lay*
*In leaves no step had trodden black.*
*Oh, I marked the first for another day!*
*Yet knowing how way leads on to way*
*I doubted if I should ever come back.*

*I shall be telling this with a sigh*
*Somewhere ages and ages hence:*
*Two roads diverged in a wood, and I,*
*I took the one less traveled by,*
*And that has made all the difference.*

# 1

## THE BEGINNING

# FOLLOW YOUR DREAMS

*The way to bring the world to life*
*is to find what brings you alive and chase it.*
— JOSEPH CAMPBELL —

Dreams are like visions.

Sometimes they happen while you're sleeping. Sometimes they happen when you're reading a book. Sometimes they happen when a loved one dies. Sometimes they happen when you're sitting in your umpteenth corporate meeting. Sometimes they happen when you're talking to someone. Sometimes they happen when you're ten years old. Sometimes they happen when you're sixty years old. Sometimes they happen in the shower. Sometimes they happen while singing along to Roy Orbison in your car. Sometimes they happen when you have your first child.

Sometimes they happen for no reason at all other than destiny.

The point is not how your vision appeared; the point is that you have the good fortune of having a vision. Not everyone is that lucky.

Maybe your dream is to have children. Maybe it's to live on an island. Maybe it's to build a billion-dollar business. Maybe it's to change the education system. Maybe it's to go to Mars.

Whatever it is, don't take it for granted. Treasure it.

Most people are milling through life with no idea where to go. Most people wish they had a dream.

If you have a dream, you're already blessed with more than most. You now have to chase it.

"I can't; I don't have enough money."

"I can't; my wife won't let me."

"I can't; it's too hard."

Blah blah blah. Excuses will only result in you lying in your bed when you're seventy years old, regretting that you never followed your dream. It's about then that you'll realize you only get one life, so maybe you should have lived it to the max.

Need money? Save up.

Spouse won't let you? Leave him or her; he or she obviously doesn't love you.

Too difficult? Toughen up.

Not only will you always regret not chasing your dreams, you're also insulting all those people out there who never had a vision, never had something to chase. They would give anything to have a dream, and yet you think it's okay to selfishly ignore yours?

Don't be a fool. Ignore the naysayers, and take the first steps to living your life to the fullest, bringing your dreams to fruition, and making the most of your short time on Earth. Yet, folks still don't do it. They consciously ignore what their heart tells them to do. Why don't people follow their dreams?

For most people, it's because they can't handle the uncertainty. Maybe this is you. Maybe you just can't handle not knowing what will happen tomorrow. So, instead of following your dream and venturing into the unknown, you choose the well-trodden path.

You choose to stay with your spouse because it's embarrassing to admit you made a mistake, even though you're desperately unhappy.

You choose your corporate job because you need the monthly salary to cover your mortgage, car payments, and school fees, even though every day at that job is soul destroying.

You choose to study medicine because you don't want to

disappoint your parents.

You choose to live your life as it is, even though you know it's not the life you should be living.

The operative word in each of these scenarios is "choose." You choose. It's a choice. For too many, not being happy is their choice. Having regrets is your choice. Having high overheads is your choice. Having a mortgage is your choice.

Not following your dreams is also your choice. Never let it be said that you didn't make the choice to waste your short time on Earth. You can't use the excuse "But I had no choice." Not everyone has a dream, but everyone has a choice.

The choice you must make is whether you're willing to pay the price of dealing with uncertainty. Are you willing to live without debt? To drive a secondhand car? To be unconcerned about what people think? To rebel against your parents? Against society?

Are you willing to lower your lifestyle and overheads in order to make yourself less vulnerable to unpleasant surprises? If you can remove the fear of the unknown, you'll be free to follow your dreams. If you follow your dreams, you'll find success.

## DON'T FOLLOW YOUR PASSION

*First they ignore you, then they laugh at you,*
*then they fight you, then you win.*

— MAHATMA GANDHI —

Your passions are different from your dreams.

Take coffee, for example. Lots of people have a "passion" for coffee. Does that mean you should start a roastery or open a coffee shop? No. That way lies failure. Don't confuse your passions with your dreams.

Your process of attaining your life's mission is unlikely to instill deep joy along the way. It will be a struggle. The reason you have this mission is because no one else wants to do it. The reason no one wants to do it is because it's not easy. Save your "passions" for the weekends.

# LOVE LIFE

*If the work you're doing is the work you're doing because you love it, then it's the right work.*

— JOSEPH CAMPBELL —

Have you ever felt that your life is great? That your work is great? That your country is great? Yet, when you tell other people, they look at you as though you're crazy.

"Dude, how can you love your life? Look at all the problems you have."

After enough repetition, you can almost start believing the skeptics. In spite of the fact that you love your life, your work, and your country, what if the crowd is right?

Maybe it's all a mess, and I should be unhappy, you think.

Stop it! Ignore the crowd. If you feel happy or blessed or lucky, then you are. It doesn't matter what other people think. It only matters that you love every day of your life. If you can't find a life that you love, then love the life you have.

# KEEP MOVING

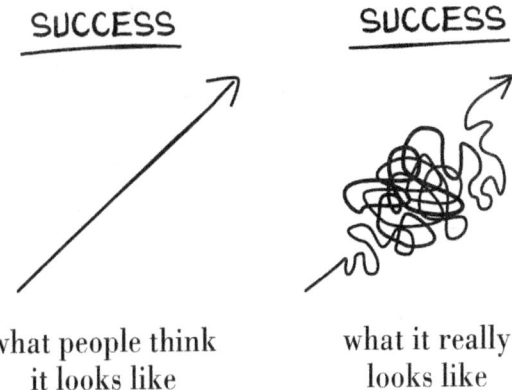

SUCCESS

what people think
it looks like

SUCCESS

what it really
looks like

Every successful person in the world has a story of ups and downs. You see the good stuff; you don't see the bad stuff.

Read the biographies of people like Winston Churchill, Abraham Lincoln, Nelson Mandela, and Benjamin Franklin. It turns out their trajectories were not all a straight line upward either. Most success stories look like straight lines from afar but are squiggles from upclose.

Because it looks so easy from the outside, you start feeling like the world is unfair. The world is not unfair; it just is. Setbacks are inevitable, and the struggle is made easier when you realize you're not the first to hit a sticky patch. Suck it up and push through. Keep moving.

## STOP TRYING TO SAVE THE WORLD

Okay, okay, we get it: the world is in trouble, and someone needs to save it.

Any other newsflashes? Get over yourself. Stop being the hero who saves the world. Be the hero who saves yourself. When you're safe, then it's time to think of your family. When your family is safe, then worry about the world. You can't help anyone before you help yourself.

Help yourself, and you help the world.

# "Lessons from a Frog"

BY OLIVIER CLERC

Put a frog in a vessel of water and start heating the water.

As the temperature of the water rises, the frog is able to adjust its body temperature accordingly.

As the water gets hotter, the frog keeps on adjusting.

Just when the water is about to reach boiling point, the frog is not able to adjust anymore.

The frog tries to jump out of the pot but is unable to do so. It has lost all its strength in adjusting to the rising water temperature.

Very soon, the frog dies.

What killed the frog?

Some would say the boiling water.

But the truth is—what killed the frog was its own inability to decide when it had to jump out.

You need to adjust to life's situations. Get the timing wrong, and splat. You're an exploded frog.

There are times when you must face the truth.

If you allow someone to exploit you physically, mentally, emotionally, or financially, he or she will continue to do so.

You have to decide when to jump.

It's your life. It's your choice.

# DO YOUR BEST

**Advice from Charles Bukowski:**

If you're going to try, go all the way.

Otherwise, don't even start.

This could mean losing girlfriends, wives, relatives, and maybe even your mind.

It could mean not eating for three or four days.

It could mean freezing on a park bench.

It could mean jail. It could mean derision.

It could mean mockery—isolation. Isolation is the gift.

All the others are a test of your endurance and of how much you really want to do it.

And you'll do it, despite rejection and the worst odds.

And it will be better than anything else you can imagine.

If you're going to try, go all the way. There is no other feeling like that.

You will be alone with the gods, and the nights will flame with fire.

You will ride life straight to perfect laughter.

It's the only good fight there is.

# VALUES

# BE LOYAL

What is loyalty?

It is having your partner's back. Always.

It is going into battle knowing that the person on your right and the person on your left are with you. You can move forward without the fear of being stabbed from behind. Loyalty is important not in its everyday presence—it is important in its absence. Loyalty is important on that one dark day when your back is against the wall and you need a friend.

If life were a walk in a rose garden, loyalty would not be an issue. "Every man for himself" is a winning motto when things are easy. Life is not a rose garden. Be loyal.

# BE RESPECTFUL

Treat everyone with equal respect. It doesn't matter if he or she is a cleaner, a CEO, a homeless person, or a billionaire; everyone has a story you can learn from. Everyone is entitled to a greeting and a smile. Pay special respect to your elders.

# TAKE RESPONSIBILITY

*Don't go around saying the world owes you a living.*
*The world owes you nothing. It was here first.*
— MARK TWAIN —

Own your problems. Own your destiny. Own your actions. Never blame others or make excuses or look for shortcuts.

It's your life; take responsibility for it.

# PERSEVERE

*Every artist was first an amateur.*
— RALPH WALDO EMERSON —

Once you've chosen your path, never give up. Keep grinding away, overcome all obstacles, and leave the pack in your dust.

Persevere.

# DO THE RIGHT THING

*When I do good, I feel good;*

*when I do bad, I feel bad, and that is my religion.*

— ABRAHAM LINCOLN —

Before you can do the right thing, you must avoid doing the wrong thing.

If you can't face your kids reading about what you do, you're doing the wrong thing. If it doesn't align with your values, you're doing the wrong thing.

If you can't tell your friends about it, you're doing the wrong thing.

What is the right thing? It's easy. Just ask yourself, "Will this action help other people?" If so, do it. If not, don't do it.

Doing the right thing is often easy, but sometimes it's really hard. Sometimes it means a bit of pain in the short run. Sometimes you need to cut ties with a friend who's holding you back. Sometimes you have to return the sweets your child shoplifted. Sometimes you have to be hard.

As cheesy as values sound, this is where they help. If you've spent time defining the ethical framework of your life, then navigating the right decisions is easier. Figure out what type of person you want to be, and from there, you'll know the right thing to do.

Do the right thing, and you'll have no regrets.

# UNDERPROMISE

Trust is the glue of life. Without trust, everything falls apart.

The surest way to lose trust is to break your promises. Instead, keep your promises. The easiest way to keep promises is to underpromise. That way you can overdeliver.

When you know you're going to break a promise, man up. Tell the truth. Take it on the chin. People will forgive overexuberance, but people will never forgive lies.

The simplest way to keep your promises is to underpromise.

# BE HUMBLE

*Arrogance is like salt. Too much ruins the pizza.*

*Too little and you lose the flavour.*

— Sam Moleshiaa —

Not only does arrogance blind you to learning lessons, but it makes enemies. No one likes arrogance. Remind yourself how lucky you have been. Also be sure to reflect upon how small you are in the big scheme of things. Be humble.

*Knowledge will give you power, but character, respect.*

— BRUCE LEE —

# 3

# CHARACTER

# SEVEN ATTRIBUTES
# OF AN ENTREPRENEUR

### 1. Be Hungry

Are you hungry? No matter how much talent you have, if you're not hungry to get ahead, you will go nowhere. Distinguish between good ambition ("I'm going to do all it takes to get ahead in life, within the bounds of morality and ethics") and evil ambition ("I'm going to do all it takes to get ahead in life, regardless of how I get there").

Good ambition values teamwork and integrity. Bad ambition ends in jail.

### 2. Love What You Do

Love what you're doing!

Wake up before the alarm clock goes off. Be excited to get to the office. Believe in the fundamental importance of your work and that it is done for the betterment of the world. If you don't love what you do, change your job. If you can't change your job, change your attitude.

### 3. Have Integrity

You must never doubt your own integrity — ever. Look at yourself in the mirror every day and ask whether you mind what your family might read about you and what you do in the newspapers.

### 4. Keep Learning

There is no substitute for sheer know-how. Don't stop learning. Surround yourself with clever people, read books, find mentors, and never stop growing your brain.

### 5. Be Open to Feedback

Without constructive criticism, analysis, and debate, it is impossible to reach the best solution to any problem. People who are willing to speak up when they disagree will help you in life. People who speak for the sake of speaking should be shot.

### 6. Have Empathy

Emotional intelligence refers to your ability to put yourself in other people's shoes. Walk a mile in the other person's shoes, and you'll probably be the same as the other person. Do unto others as you would have them do unto you.

### 7. Be Quiet

If you have nothing to say, don't say anything.

# BE EQUANIMOUS

When one is equanimous, he or she has the ability to react to good and bad news the same way. It means being cool regardless of what happens.

Here are some tips for cultivating equanimity in yourself.

- See the world as it is, rather than as you want it to be.
- Look for the positive in every negative.
- Accept that things always change.
- Don't take things personally.
- Practice breathing deeply.
- Meditate or pray.
- Be grateful.

You'll have some victories, so go ahead and celebrate. Just don't let it go to your head. When you experience defeats, don't panic and don't whine.

Control what you can, and accept what you can't. Be cool. Keep moving.

# HAVE A SENSE OF HUMOR

*If I had no sense of humour,*
*I would long ago have committed suicide.*

— MAHATMA GANDHI —

## 1. Laugh at Yourself

Your greatest potential enemy is your ego. The surefire telltale of someone whose ego is out of control is an inability to laugh at himself or herself.

The moment you take yourself too seriously, you set yourself up for failure. Always have humility. That way you have an open mind and can absorb feedback. You will take risks along the way, and you will fail along the way. You will regularly seem foolish along the way, and if you can't laugh at yourself, you're screwed.

Don't take yourself too seriously.

## 2. Laugh at Setbacks

*A person without a sense of humour*
*is like a wagon without springs.*
*It's jolted by every pebble on the road.*

— HENRY WARD BEECHER —

Sometimes your bets won't pay off. If you can't laugh off your setbacks, you'll soon stop taking risks. If you stop taking risks, you'll stop learning.

If you stop learning, why are you here?

### 3. Laugh at Fear

Fear — of failure, of losing money, of embarrassment, of rejection — will be a major challenge in your life.

Overcome your fears so you can keep moving forward. The easiest way to overcome your fears is to laugh at them. Laugh at death. So, you die. So what?

When you're dead, it doesn't matter.

### 4. Make Other People Laugh

Most people don't want to know the truth. You can either bulldoze your story into their brains or tell a joke that subtly plants the seed. Oscar Wilde recommended the latter: "If you want to tell people the truth, make them laugh, otherwise they'll kill you."

Regardless of whether you take risks in your life, sometimes the universe throws you lemons. It can seem unfair that you have acne, nonexistent calves, an unwelcoming school, poor parents (or no parents), or whatever.

Bad stuff happens. Most of what happens in life, good or bad, is a function of the postal code in which you were born. You had no say in that. Most of life is random. You got lucky or unlucky.

If you look at the funny side of life, it's easier to laugh off the bad luck.

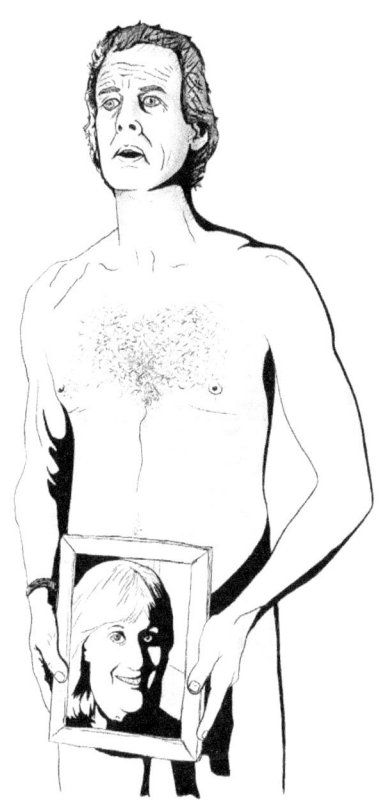

*Do you have any idea what it's like being English? Being so correct all the time, being so stifled by this dread of doing the wrong thing, or saying to someone, "Are you married?" and hearing, "My wife left me this morning," or saying, "Do you have children?" and being told they all burned to death on Wednesday.*

*You see, we're all terrified of embarrassment.*

— JOHN CLEESE —
from A FISH CALLED WANDA

# THERE IS NO TRY; THERE IS ONLY DO

*Do. Or do not. There is no try.*

— YODA —
from THE EMPIRE STRIKES BACK

"I tried my best" is a line for losers. It's a line for a world where someone will bail you out, where you can use excuses to cover failure, where you can blame others, and where you don't need to worry about consequences.

Entrepreneurs don't live in that world. Entrepreneurs know that "try" is a meaningless verb. Entrepreneurs know there is no bailout, no one to catch them, and no plan B.

Entrepreneurs know that there is only one way: to survive and thrive.

That way is to do, not to try.

# MAKE IT LOOK EASY

We all have a friend who works damn hard. You don't even need to ask him or her—that person will tell you. "Blah blah blah."

Toughen up. Everyone works hard, everyone makes sacrifices, and everyone puts in the hours. Who cares if people think you work hard? The only thing that matters is that you deliver the goods. Sometimes that means getting up at four o'clock in the morning. Sometimes it means working eighty-hour weeks. Sometimes it means being on the road for months at a time. Don't complain, don't fish for compliments or commiseration, and don't make a big deal about it. When you're working hard, you should behave the same as when you're on holiday. "Never been better!"

So what if some people think you're lazy or you have it easy? It doesn't matter what people say. It only matters what people do. The appearance of working hard is a crutch. It's a disguise for not delivering the goods. "But I put in the hours," you might say. "It's not my fault I didn't win." No one cares.

No one will bail you out. Whether you put in the hours or not, there is no mercy and no mitigating circumstances. If you don't deliver the goods, you fail.

It's easy to make it look hard. It takes a lot of effort to make it look effortless.

Make it look easy.

## GO THE EXTRA MILE

Some people finish the day and think, Have I done as much as I can get away with today?

These people are not entrepreneurs.

An entrepreneur finishes the day and thinks, Is there anything else I can do today?

If you want a successful life, you need an edge. You need to be doing stuff other people aren't doing. You need to be learning stuff other people aren't learning. You need to be working longer hours.

An entrepreneur leaves no stone unturned. He or she knows failure is not an option. No one else will do the work. Entrepreneurs go the extra mile every day because they know the extra mile is never crowded.

# GIVE IT YOUR BEST SHOT!
# NO EXCUSES

Some people are so afraid of losing that they don't get into the race. Maybe you're one of them.

You've been told your whole life you're a winner. You've always beaten your friends and your enemies. You've always been first in class. You were a prefect—and then you entered the real world. As it turns out, the real world doesn't teach you lessons before the test. The real world gives you the test and then teaches you a lesson.

"It's so unfair! How can I be sure I'll win if I don't know what to expect?"

Imagine losing. People will think you're a loser. All those friends of yours who you've silently looked down upon might now silently look down upon you. Better not to try, you rationalize. Better to fake an injury and pull out. Better to stand on the sidelines saying, "Oh, woe is me! If only I wasn't injured. I'm so much better than these guys."

That way, no one can say you're a loser. You just had bad luck.

That is not how you become a hero. Life entails taking risk. It means venturing into the unknown. It means maybe not coming first in your class. Park your ego, step into the ring, and give it your best, even if that means learning that your peers are better than you.

Life is not about what other people think—or more importantly, what you think. Life is about giving it your best shot and having no regrets.

# HELP OTHER PEOPLE

*Feed the stream of life, not your own dam.*

— Francois van Niekerk —

Remember when you used to hitchhike? You'd stand by the side of the road for hours, waiting for someone to pick you up. Maybe you have a car now, and maybe you see hitchhikers by the road. Do you pick them up?

Always help other people, even when times are tough for you. Who knows? Maybe that person in need will one day help you. Regardless of whether there is a chance of payback, help other people if you can. When you're in a position of power, it's easy to forget how desperate you can feel when you're trying to make it in life, when you're standing by the side of the road.

Never forget: always help other people when you can.

# MAKE HASTE SLOWLY

*Only the God-less run when no one is chasing them.*

— KING SOLOMON —

Festina lente was the motto for Augustus, the last great emperor of Rome. It means "make haste slowly." He was not a dude known for hesitation, but he understood the dangers of being overly hasty.

Before firing the laser, ask yourself, "Is this decision important?" If it's not important, go ahead and make a decision. The consequences will be minor if it's the wrong call, and you can quickly change course. If it's a big decision, pause.

Sleep on big decisions. Your subconscious will deal with the question while you sleep, and when you wake up, you'll know what the right thing is. Sometimes it's so complicated you need a few nights to sleep on it. Take your time. Anyone who won't let you have a couple of nights to think about something is an ass. Don't let anyone force a quick decision on you.

Make haste slowly.

# TELL THE TRUTH

*If you want to tell people the truth,*
*make them laugh, otherwise they'll kill you.*

— OSCAR WILDE —

It's easy to fib, to tell a white lie so as not to hurt someone's feelings. It's easy to say the politically correct thing, but it's a slippery slope that ends in sleepless nights.

If you want to be successful, tell the truth. You will attract the right kind of people and repel the wrong kind of people. You will sleep easily at night. Telling the truth means you don't have to remember what you said.

It's not easy to speak the truth, especially to power. Many people will tell you to tone it down, to be diplomatic, or to be sensitive. Ignore these people.

They're mostly well-meaning, but they are taking you away from your single most important life mission: being yourself.

Telling the truth doesn't mean being disrespectful or rude or that it's acceptable to hurt people. That's where skill comes in. It's an art to tell people the way it is without offending them. It's an art worth learning, unless you want to be beaten up (figuratively and literally).

Sometimes the best thing to do is leave the conversation. If the audience isn't interested, don't spend energy shining a light on the truth. Move on to people with open minds. Tell the truth. If you can't tell the truth, you're wasting your life.

# NEVER LIE

It's easy to lie, especially when you have the gift of gab. Here are some tricks to stop yourself from lying:

## 1. Don't Keep Secrets

Be known as the person who never keeps a secret. When a friend or a stranger tells you a secret, immediately tell everyone you know—and thereby make people think twice before they tell you a secret.

Secrets are bad. When people tell you a secret, they make you an accomplice to a lie. Eventually, a situation will arise when you're asked a straight question, and if you are to keep the secret, you must lie. You'll be a liar.

Rather, stay clear of secrets. Who cares if your friends don't want to tell you secrets? It's better to never have to lie.

## 2. One-Reason Rule

Nassim Taleb has a great trick for avoiding self-rationalization:

If you need more than one reason, you're rationalizing.

If you're rationalizing, you're lying.

If you can't find one reason that's good enough to do something, don't do it.

## 3. Don't Use Passwords

Don't use a password for your phone or laptop. Leave your stuff lying around so people can access it. When you have no locked devices, you'll quickly ensure that you have no secrets to hide.

## 4. The Internet Means There Are No More Secrets

Speak and behave as though everyone will eventually know

what you said and did. The Internet is here. There are no more secrets.

If you lie, you will eventually be caught out.

## 5. Live in a Small Town

There are no secrets in a small community.

## 6. Avoid Bad People

If you hang with the wrong crowd, you will eventually be forced to cover for them and become an accomplice in their bad acts.

## 7. Walk in the Middle of the Street

Always bring witnesses to important meetings. Don't be dragged into a room alone. Avoid temptation. Walk in the middle of the street where everyone can see you.

# MAXIMIZE YOUR ENERGY

Energy is everything. It is what keeps us moving forward and what makes us optimistic. Energy is what takes you forward in life, and it's what attracts the right kind of people or the wrong kind of people. Ignore money, ignore time, and focus on energy.

There are four kinds of energy you need to maximize.

## 1. Physical Energy

Sleep six hours a day. Eat healthily. Stay away from sugar. Exercise every day; twenty minutes is all you need to be a hero.

## 2. Mental Energy

Read, write, reflect, and come up with new ideas every day. Exercise your mind, and your mind will become more energetic.

## 3. Emotional Energy

Steer clear of negative emotions like envy, pride, and anger. Focus on positive emotions like gratitude, humility, and happiness. Steer clear of people who drag you down. Hang out with people who give you energy. When you feel yourself losing control of your emotions, don't panic. Breathe slowly and smile.

## 4. Spiritual Energy

Pray, meditate, and go for long walks. Find a purpose that's bigger than you: kids, religion, country, or whatever. Victor Frankl, an Austrian neurologist, psychiatrist, and Holocaust survivor, explained that those who survived the Nazi concentration camps were living for something or someone else. Those who lived only for themselves soon gave up and died.

# THIRTEEN THINGS AN ENTREPRENEUR DOESN'T DO

1. Lie
2. Panic
3. Judge others
4. Drink Frisco
5. Put ice in red wine
6. Neglect their family
7. Add sugar to coffee
8. Tell tales on colleagues
9. Drink wine out of a box
10. Drive when they can walk
11. Believe what they read in newspapers
12. Treat the cleaner differently than the CEO
13. Fly business class when they can fly economy

# 4

# PHILOSOPHY

# BE ANTIFRAGILE

Nassim Taleb's book Antifragile is a bible for entrepreneurs.

The theory is to set up your life in such a way that not only are you resilient to shocks, but you actually benefit when adversity strikes. One of the best examples he uses is debt. Debt makes you fragile. If interest rates go up or the bank calls in your loan, you're in trouble. Not having debt makes you resilient. Having lots of cash makes you antifragile.

Being antifragile means devising a strategy whereby you benefit from unpleasant shocks to the system, like when you can't find decent coffee. Are you the person who simply won't drink coffee unless it's excellent? The problem with that strategy is that you are vulnerable to painful shocks when in a strange town and unable to find great coffee (e.g., in all towns between Cape Town and Johannesburg).

It's time to change tack! Start drinking instant coffee again. When you start liking it again, you'll be antifragile to coffee. If there's great coffee available, that's awesome! If there's only Ricoffy, that's awesome too! (Thank you, Nassim Taleb.)

Here are some other tips for antifragility:

- Stick to simple rules.
- Keep your options open.
- Don't get consumed by the data.
- Resist the urge to suppress randomness.
- Experiment and tinker.
- Take lots of small risks.
- Make sure you have your soul in the game.
- Avoid bets that, if lost, would wipe you out completely.
- Build in redundancy and layers. Have no single point of

failure.

- Respect history; look for habits and rules that have been around for a long time.
- Focus more on avoiding things that don't work than trying to find out what does work.

When adversity strikes, you should not only survive but also thrive. Set your life up in such a way that no matter what happens, you benefit. It's a form of opportunism; everything that happens—good or bad—creates opportunity.

You want to be in a position to be able to take advantage of any opportunities that arise, and that means having cash in hand. It also means loving what you do.

Sometimes you simply can't avoid failure, but if you love what you do, you haven't wasted your time. No matter whether you win or lose, you've benefited. If you love what you do, you're antifragile.

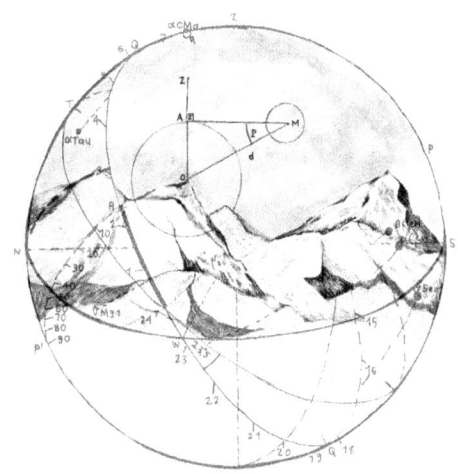

# BE STOIC

Stoicism is a philosophy that was built for hard times. What better philosophy for an entrepreneur?

The key pillars of stoicism are as follows:

- Your principles are more important than your wealth, health, and reputation.
- Emotions such as anger and fear are personal choices.
- Focus on what is within your control.
- Don't react to others.

Being stoic doesn't mean being hard-hearted or unemotional. "Free from passions" doesn't mean you should live like a statue. Although external things are beyond your direct control, you must nevertheless try to take appropriate action to increase your odds of success. You will be affected by your emotions, but by employing the virtues of courage and self-discipline, you will not be carried away by your feelings.

As a stoic, you realize that you can only act to the best of your ability. At some point, the result is out of your hands. Whatever happens will happen. Not only should you accept your fate but you should embrace it. Amor fati (love fate) is your goal.

What counts is your intent. Was your initial action made under your rational control, or were you acting out of passion?

Did you act for the right reasons, or were you motivated by negative emotions?

The answers to these questions will determine whether you have done the right thing.

One thousand years ago, Christians used to write Deo Volente" at the end of letters. It means "God willing" in Latin. Muslims say Insha'Allah, Arabic for "God willing."

Times haven't changed that much. Do your best, but if things don't go your way, remind yourself that what is meant to be will be.

Here are some basic rules for a stoic life.

## 1. Focus on What You Can Control

Distinguish between things that are under your control and things that are not. Don't let yourself be upset by things over which you have no influence, such as other people and external events. Rather, focus on yourself and your own behavior. Your actions and choices are under your own control.

*Demand not that events should happen as you wish;*

*but wish them to happen as they do happen,*
*and your life will be serene.*

— EPICTETUS —

## 2. Find a Role Model

Decide what kind of person you want to be. Set some principles and routines you want to follow, and then find a role model who exemplifies this path.

It's not easy, but with small steps and adjustments for mishaps, you can become closer to the character you wish to have.

## 3. Be Equanimous

Handle success and disaster in the same manner. Train yourself to be indifferent to reputation, wealth, and health. This doesn't mean that you should have no feelings or emotions. Rather, you should not let your feelings or emotions control you. Being able to remain above your base instincts starts with being able to control your reaction to events.

## 4. Align Yourself and the World

Know yourself. Then understand the world. Then align yourself with the world. If you can align your path with the world, you will find success.

## 5. Don't Waste Your Life

You only have one life to live. Do not postpone your dreams and your happiness.

Every minute of every day should be dedicated toward attaining happiness. If that means working in a coal mine to save enough money to retire to the beach, so be it. If you can't choose work that you love, love the work you do.

## 6. Treat the Obstacle as the Way

As Ryan Holiday brilliantly explains in his book The Obstacle in the Path Becomes the Path, embrace adversity and challenges, for they will make you stronger and differentiate you from the chasing pack.

## 7. Be Present

It's easy to be caught up in reflection on the past or anticipation of the future. Don't.

Focus on the present—today, right now. Don't look at your phone when seeing people. Pay attention to your surroundings. Do one thing at a time. Focus. Stay in the moment, and the future will take care of itself.

## 8. Never Stop Moving

There is only one thing worse than going backward in life: staying where you are.

Don't procrastinate. Keep moving. You can't grow if you don't encounter new things and take on new challenges. When you're finding yourself bored or frozen, that's the time to get worried. The stoics understood that we only have one life. Don't waste it.

## DEALING WITH UNCERTAINTY

If you want to have a life of adventure, you need to become

comfortable with not knowing what's going to happen tomorrow. You need to be comfortable with uncertainty. Do everything you can to increase your tolerance for uncertainty. Put yourself in a position where there is no such thing as "an unpleasant surprise." Make all surprises pleasant. Here are some tricks to getting comfortable with uncertainty.

## 1. Do Not Care What People Think

Make yourself immune to the opinions of the crowd. The way to do this is to embarrass yourself regularly in public. If you always seem perfect, your ego will become brittle, and you will develop a deep fear of public failure. Rather, get into the habit of doing things outside your comfort zone, like public speaking or singing or anything that makes you cringe. Cringing is the cure for fear of humiliation. After enough cringes, you'll be immunized.

## 2. Have a Safety Net

Don't leap from the cliff unless you have a safety net. If you're lucky enough to have been born into a wealthy family, good for you. If not, you have two options: marry rich or start saving.

If your venture doesn't generate money as fast as you think it will (it won't), your safety net will save you from hitting the ground with a splat.

### 3. Live a Simple Life

The most important tool for taking risk is to live a simple life. Don't be ostentatious and drive a flashy car. Keep your overheads low, regardless of your income. Keeping your life simple has benefits other than allowing you to take risk.

a) You'll avoid the wrong spouse. It's easier to attract the right spouse if you're not driving a Ferrari. Do you really want to marry the kind of person who finds a fancy car irresistible?

b) You'll avoid temptation. The high life brings temptations to go to the dark side. Why test your resolve? You have enough on your plate making your life a success. Rather, avoid temptation. A simple life keeps you away from doing bad stuff.

c) You'll extend your runway. If you keep your personal overhead low, then your runway gets longer and you can plug away at your dreams for longer. High overhead equals short runway.

d) You'll think clearly. How can you think clearly when you're constantly surrounded by your courtiers and cars and houses and stuff? The fewer distractions you have in your life, the more you can focus your mental energy on success.

You can't take any of your assets and trophies with you when you die. When you die, you're dead. You're dust. All the material goods are meaningless. The only meaningful thing is whether you left a positive impact on the world during your short time alive.

### 4. Control Your Reactions

Your life story is not a series of events. It's a series of your reactions to events. Don't let your successes and failures define you. What defines you is your reaction to success and failure. Be humble in victory and be positive in failure.

Control your reactions.

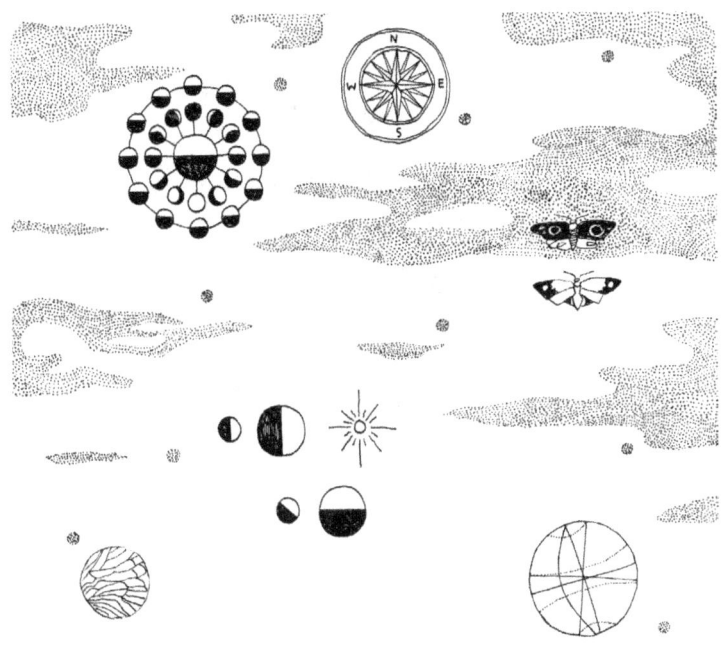

## DON'T BE FOOLED
## BY RANDOMNESS

Sometimes bad stuff happens. Sometimes good stuff happens. It's not your fault, nor is it to your credit. If your business fails due to a global financial recession, it's not your fault. Your failure was random. Don't take it personally.

If your house price goes up due to a global property boom, you're not a genius. Your success was random, so don't let it go to your head.

Some things are within your control, but most things are not. Be cool. React equally to disaster and triumph. Accept that life can be random, starting with where you are born. No one owes you anything, and no one is out to get you. Play the hand you're dealt. Don't be fooled by randomness.

# THIRTEEN RULES FOR HAPPINESS

*When I was five years old, my mother always told me that happiness was the key to life. When I went to school, they asked me what I wanted to be when I grew up. I wrote down "happy." They told me I didn't understand the assignment, and I told them they didn't understand life."*

— JOHN LENNON —

1. Don't be upset when wronged. Let bad deeds flow over you like water.

2. If someone has a problem with you, that's his or her problem.

3. Keep an eye on the big picture. Think of how small your problems are in the bigger scheme of things.

4. Share your problems. You'll find others return the favor,

and you'll quickly realize you're not alone and your problems aren't so bad.

5. Avoid unhappy people. Only spend time with people who exude positive energy.

6. Are you an introvert? If so, make time to be by yourself and recharge your batteries.

7. Are you an extrovert? If so, make time to socialize and recharge your batteries.

8. Marry the right person. There is no substitute for coming home to someone who loves you, regardless of the challenges in your life.

9. Have kids. They will make you appreciate little things (like a good night's sleep).

10. Don't read the papers. Ignorance truly is bliss. The only information you need is on stuff over which you can exert some control. As for the rest? Forget about it.

11. Exercise for twenty minutes every day. Walking is exercise.

12. Stay clear of sugar. It gives you a temporary energy spike but brings an inevitable downer. Sugar also suppresses your immune system, which makes you more vulnerable to getting sick.

13. Stay close to your family and friends. The stronger your community ties and relationships, the happier you'll be.

## CONTROL YOUR DESTINY

It's easy to go through life believing you have no control over events. "Keep your head down," you're told. "Take no risks, stay alive, and accept things the way they are." It's called "blowing with the wind," and some people have perfected the art.

These are the people who sit in meetings and always look to the person with power. "What do they want?" They look at the group consensus and make sure they're with it. Regardless of promises or decisions made before the meeting, they go with the crowd. These people are afraid. They're afraid of taking responsibility for their decisions, their careers, and their lives. They don't want to have control. They want to follow.

An entrepreneur is not like this. While she acknowledges that the world is enormous and complicated, she also refuses to accept that she can't nudge it in the direction she wants. She never avoids the truth. She never follows the crowd. She never accepts things just because "that's the way things are." She grabs the bull by the horns, lives her life the way she wants to, and accepts the consequences. She exerts her will on reality and expects reality to change.

An entrepreneur takes responsibility for her business, her happiness, and her life. She refuses to accept that everything is fate. She might have to accept her destiny, but she'll have a say in what her destiny is. Life doesn't happen to her—she happens to life.

Take control of your own destiny.

# LISTEN TO THE UNIVERSE

*If you come to a fork in the road, take it.*

— YOGI BERRA —

Every day, you get signals and signs telling you whether you're on the right track (or the wrong track); pay attention.

The universe is taking you somewhere. If you pay attention, you can get there without unnecessary resistance. Picture yourself as a wave. If you go against the current, you dissipate and disappear. If you go across the current, you get messed up by other waves. The biggest waves go with the current. If you want to be the biggest wave and make the biggest splash, go with the current. Go with the universe.

Maybe your mission is to find love. Say your heart is set on a girl. You're putting all your energy into winning her, but she's making the chase difficult. Yet the girl of your dreams is right beside you, under your nose. "Choose me! Choose me!" If you're not paying attention, you'll end up with the wrong life partner.

Maybe your mission is to raise money. You think you know where to look, but in spite of frantic searching, you are without success. Calm down, make sure people know what you need, and wait for the help to come to you. Maybe no one gives you capital. Maybe someone calls out of the blue and saves the day. That's the universe helping you out, either by ensuring you don't raise money to go down a dead end or that you don't bring the wrong shareholder on board.

Everything happens for a reason. Work as hard as you possibly can, but then have the patience to stop and read the signs and signals that are before you every day. A false path in life is something you are attracted to for the wrong reasons—money, fame, attention, and so on. Filter out those motives.

Listen to the universe.

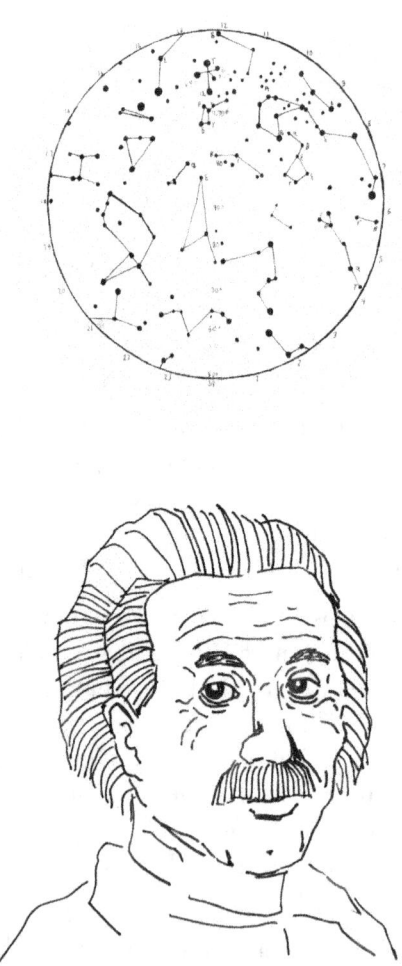

# 5

# SELF-AWARENESS

*Don't let the world squash your cheesiness.*

— BRAND PRETORIUS —

# KNOW THYSELF

*I yam what I yam.*

— Popeye —

You must be yourself. You can only be yourself if you know yourself.

You can only know yourself if you keep pushing your limits, keep taking risks, keep falling, and keep getting up again. Most people know how to handle good times. The trick is knowing how to handle the bad times. Not only do you need to know how you handle adversity, you need to know how the people around you handle adversity.

What will your wife do if you lose your money and have to start again? What will your friends do if you have an embarrassing setback?

What will your investors do if you lose their money?

Life is too short to spend time with people who will abandon you. The better you know who you are, the easier it is to attract the kind of people who will stick by you through thick and thin.

Know yourself, and you'll find your tribe.

# KNOW WHAT YOU DON'T KNOW

*All I know is that I know nothing.*

— Socrates —

If you want to know what your strengths are, you need to start by learning what your weaknesses are: what you're not good at, what you don't know, and what you don't have experience in doing.

Sometimes success leads to an overinflated estimation of your abilities. Sometimes you just don't know yourself. Stay humble. Look in the mirror and see yourself for who you truly are. Once you've discovered the gap in your knowledge and experience, you can look for the people who complement you.

# KNOW YOUR MOTIVES

Do you know why you do what you do? Is it the money? Is it the fame? Is it the power? Is it the girls? Is it the boys? Is it to save the world? Is it because you can't get a job?

The reason doesn't matter. The only thing that matters is that you're honest with yourself. Knowing why you do something is important when times are tough and you want to quit. If you don't know why you're doing something, you'll give up.

# USE YOUR NATURAL GIFTS

"The Sword of Truth" series by Terry Goodkind is a story about a woods guide who is tasked with a quest to save the world. He accepts out of a sense of responsibility but feels wholly inadequate and is convinced he's the wrong man for the job.

Throughout the story, he repeatedly performs unbelievable feats of magic while simultaneously refusing to believe that he has magic. After a while, the novelty of his modesty wears off, and the reader starts thinking, Get over yourself. You have magic; you are a wizard. Deal with it!

Eventually, he accepts that he is a wizard, but when he finds himself using his magic too much, he begins to feels that he is becoming a slave to his own powers. In the nick of time, he pulls back from the edge and learns to control his urges, realizing that the secret is a combination of confidence and humility.

This is the story of life.

**You have three options:**

1. Lifelong denial of your talents, unhappy life, and death.

2. Initial denial of your talents, acceptance, overconfidence, explosion, and death.

3. Initial denial of your talents, acceptance, overconfidence, humility, balance, and death.

It's a choice. Stop denying your talent. Go out there and use it.

# YOUR REPUTATION
# DOESN'T MATTER

*Pay no attention to the critics. Don't even ignore them.*

— SAMUEL GOLDWYN —

While reputation can be a useful tool in life, in the final analysis, it simply doesn't matter what people think about you. It only matters what you think about you.

What you think about yourself is entirely dependent on what you do. If you do nothing, then you're nothing, and the crowd won't care anyway.

If you do something meaningful, then you're meaningful, and who cares what the crowd thinks?

Basing your actions upon your reputation is dangerous and can lead you down a path that is not your path. Instead of doing the right thing for your life, you'll end up doing the right thing for your reputation. You'll end up living according to what other people think. Someone who will do anything to protect his reputation will eventually ruin his reputation. Forget your reputation. Do the right thing.

*Dogs only bark at moving cars.*

— JASON NGOBENI —

# FOCUS ON YOUR TALENTS

Warren Buffett has an approach for how you can identify your greatest talents and maximize your focus. It's called the Two-List Process.

**Step 1:** Write down the list of your top twenty-five talents.

**Step 2:** Circle the top five items on this list.

**Step 3:** You will now have two lists (List A consisting of the five circled talents and List B consisting of the remaining twenty).

Instead of treating List A as high priority and List B as low priority, treat List B as those behaviors you should avoid at all cost. No matter what, the items on your second list must get no attention from you.

**Here's how it works.**

List B (talents six to twenty-five) are things you're pretty good at. Compared to List A, however, they are distractions. It's easy spending time on the twenty things you're pretty good at. What's not easy is putting all your energy into the five things at which you excel. Focus on the talents at which you excel, and you'll become the best in the world.

# EGO IS LIKE A DRAGON

*Fairy tales are more than true: not because they tell
us that dragons exist, but because they tell us that
dragons can be beaten.*

— G. K. CHESTERTON —

In all the fairy tales of old, the hero must either slay the dragon
or tame it. The best heroes actually have a pet dragon and fly into
battle. The bigger your dragon, the more of a hero you are. The
dragon is a metaphor for ego. It's good to have a big ego, but just
like with dragons, your ego can kill you.

The solution is not to kill the ego or reduce it in size. It's to
control it. The bigger your ego (in other words, the greater your
self-assurance), the more powerful you are as an entrepreneur.
Just keep a watchful eye on it.

*Be who you are and say what you feel,
because those who mind don't matter,
and those who matter don't mind.*

— DR. SEUSS —

# HABITS

# MAKE YOUR BED IN THE MORNING

Making your bed in the morning seems stupid. You're way too important for such mundane tasks, right? You're in a rush. Someone else will do it.

Stop being a fool. When you get up in the morning, pause and make your bed. First, it's an effective trick for feeling like you've achieved something for the day. Bed made? Tick. Next. You can get your daily task ball rolling with something simple. Start every day with the momentum of knowing you've accomplished one thing already.

Second, it's an exercise in doing a job properly. Anyone can throw the duvet over the sheets and walk out the door. It takes an extra sixty seconds to straighten the sheets, puff the pillows, and square off the corners. Get into the habit of making your bed properly, and you'll find yourself doing everything else properly.

Third, it keeps you real. You want to be antifragile in life. Be resilient and self-sufficient. If you don't know how to make a bed, you're fragile. Success can suck you away from the basics. Consciously go back to basics.

Light your fire without blitz. Chop your own wood. Book your own flights.

Make your own bed.

# DON'T BE TOO PROUD
# TO DO THE DIRTY WORK

*Chop your own wood. It will warm you twice.*

— BEN FRANKLIN —

It's easy to think you're the big chief or that certain jobs are beneath you—or that parents, secretaries, and underlings were invented to take care of the detail.

It's also easy to be a loser.

A hero is never too proud to do the dirty work. He or she will do whatever it takes to win (ethically). For example, she will

- Sell
- Apologize
- Book flights
- Make coffee
- Admit failure
- Sweep the stoop
- Write the leave policy.

Park your ego and face the facts. The number-one fact is that the buck stops with you. There is no job beneath you. There is no sales pitch you can delegate. There is no room for not apologizing. There is no forgiveness for denying failure. Do what you have to do, and do it yourself. You'll be rewarded twice.

# WRITE EVERY DAY

*The best writing is rewriting.*

— E. B. White —

Get into the habit of writing every day, preferably on a public forum like a blog, where people can see it. Public writing forces you to think carefully before you publish, it gives you feedback, and it helps other people.

The habit of daily writing has the following benefits:

### 1. It Makes You More Observant

If you know you have to write something every day, you will start opening your eyes to the world around you. Desperation for content will make you pay attention to learning opportunities that previously passed unnoticed like the proverbial ship in the night.

### 2. It Forces You to Clearly Articulate Your Thinking

It's easy to talk a good game, but it's not as easy to write a good game. Writing is what separates the fuzzy heads from the clear thinkers. Writing makes you think clearly. If you can't think clearly, you can't be a hero.

### 3. It Helps You Avoid Making the Same Mistakes

In your constant search for content, you'll be forced to reflect on your personal experiences and the lessons you can extract from them. Reflecting on those lessons will increase the odds of avoiding the same mistakes.

## WAKE UP EARLY

Are you not a morning person? Do you drag yourself out of bed?

Did your mom spend years shouting at you to get up so you didn't miss the school bus? Are you convinced you need nine hours of solid sleep to be functional?

Good news:

- Waking up early is a learned habit, not a genetic trait.
- You don't need more than six hours of sleep a night.
- Your sleep can be interrupted.

These are medical facts. Google them.

Waking up early gives you an edge in life. During the hours from five to seven in the morning, it's quiet and your brain is fresh. You will have uninterrupted working time at peak creativity. Two extra hours a day equates to sixty extra hours a month—and that represents a massive time advantage over the people who sleep late.

Here are some tricks that will make it easier to wake up early.

1. **Get Married**

   Once you are married, you don't have an incentive to go out drinking and partying every night. That means you will go to bed earlier and wake up without a hangover.

2. **Start Your Own Business**

   Waking up early to make money for someone else can be difficult. Waking up early to make money for yourself? Easy— especially if you love what you do.

3. **Love What You Do**

   When you love what you do, you won't find it hard to get out of bed.

4. **Have Children**

   Kids will recalibrate your expectations for how much sleep

you need.

When your two-year-old wakes you up at 4:30 a.m., and you spend thirty minutes getting her back to sleep, you can either try and go back to bed or open your laptop and start working.

If you want to succeed in life, you need every edge you can get. Either stick to your mantra of "I'm not a morning person" or follow the advice of Benjamin Franklin: "Early to bed, early to rise, makes a man healthy, wealthy, and wise."

## HAVE GOOD MANNERS

It never hurts to have good manners. Open the door for ladies. Ask to take off your jacket before sitting. Offer to make coffee. Say please and thank you.

Good manners are a sign of respect, and they might give you an edge. If someone is offended by your good manners, you don't want to do business with that person. Manners help you stand out from the crowd. It's like wearing a floral shirt without actually wearing a floral shirt.

Manners garner attention; they make people sit up and notice, and they set a good example for your kids. There are a thousand reasons to have good manners and none for not having them.

Entrepreneurs have good manners.

## AVOID SMALL DECISIONS

Many of the world's greatest inventors, artists, and entrepreneurs were creatures of habit.

They realized that if they wanted to free up their creative juices and save their brain power for important matters, they had to minimize time and energy spent on repeatable tasks, such as meals, clothes, and daily chores. Steve Jobs always wore the same polo sweater and jeans. Benjamin Franklin always had the same breakfast. Leonardo da Vinci always woke up at the same time of day. Barack Obama only had two suit colors, blue and black.

By removing the need to make hundreds of small, inane decisions in the day—What should I have for breakfast? What time should I wake up? What type of coffee should I have? What should I wear today?—you minimize decision fatigue and maximize your creativity.

*Be regular and ordinary in your life so that*
*you may be violent and original in your work.*

— Gustave Flaubert —

## WASH YOUR HANDS

Not only is it unpleasant to be sick, but it's also bad for success. You can't afford to stop moving.

Here are some guidelines for staying healthy:

1. **Stay away from sugar.** Sugar is said to suppress your immune system for up to five hours.
2. **Don't get drunk.** (A drink or two is okay; a hangover is not.)
3. **Fist bump rather than shake hands.**
4. **Drink ginger tea with lemon.**
5. **Wash your hands regularly.**
6. **Don't touch your face.**
7. **Get enough sleep.**

Being sick is not an excuse for failing. Don't get sick.

# LIVE SIMPLY

*The greatest wealth is to live content with little.*

— PLATO —

Entrepreneurs need to be antifragile, resilient to setbacks, and capable of facing adversity without flinching. That's why you need a simple lifestyle.

You will be unaffected by poor fare if you don't need much. Eat All-Bran flakes for breakfast. Wear jeans, T-shirts, and sneakers. If you want to go to extremes, sleep on the floor rather than in a comfy bed. Not only does it make you resilient, but a simple lifestyle boosts your creativity by minimizing decision fatigue.

A simple lifestyle doesn't mean compromising on quality or settling for second best. It just means stripping the unnecessary stuff from your life and focusing on what's important. You can still be extraordinary. You can eat great food, send your kids to world-class schools, travel to amazing places, and create great memories.

You just don't need a Ferrari.

# SMILE AND WAVE

Develop a small circle of trust. Within that circle, you can share your trials and tribulations and be vulnerable. Outside that circle, always have your game face on. No matter how bad your day, no matter how painful or embarrassing something is, no matter what happens along the way, remember: smile and wave.

# BE A PARANOID OPTIMIST

You can't be happy unless you have a fundamentally positive view of the future. You have to be the kind of person who believes everything will turn out okay in the end.

You must be the opposite of pessimistic, but you must also be paranoid. The only way to be sure that everything will turn out okay in the end is if you're constantly looking for imminent threats and neutralizing them.

Andy Grove wrote Only the Paranoid Survive, one of the best business books ever. It tells the story of how he saved Intel in the face of massive industry disruptions. He could see the incoming threats and knew he had two choices:

1. **Do nothing and have a 0 percent chance of surviving.**
2. **Change the business and have 50 percent chance of surviving.**

He chose option two, and he saved Intel.

If you want to succeed, wake up every morning and think, What can go wrong today? Only once you're sure there are no imminent threats, you can you think of moving forward.

Be a paranoid optimist.

# NAP

Not getting enough sleep? Kids keeping you up? Too much on your mind? Struggling to keep your energy up in the afternoon?

The answer is napping. A twenty-minute power nap will lower your stress levels while boosting motor skills, creativity, and memory. Teach yourself to power nap. Have a routine, find a dark place, and make it quick. One power nap during the day means you only need six hours of sleep in the evening.

If you can be creative and energized for seventeen hours every day, you'll get an edge on your competition—and you need every edge you can get. Nap.

# MEDITATE

To some people, meditation seems a tad cheesy. Fortunately for entrepreneurs, cheesy is good. Meditation is probably the simplest way of cultivating focus, restoring energy, and managing stress.

Mindfulness meditation is widely taught to cancer patients, prisoners, and people suffering from anxiety, depression, or chronic pain. It can't be bad for you.

There are two meditation techniques.

1. **Concentration Meditation:**
   Concentrate your attention on a single point, an object, an image, an imagined sound, or the physical sensation of your own breathing.

### 2. Mindfulness Meditation:

Keep your attention rooted in the present moment, and observe your thoughts and sensations from a perspective of neutral detachment. This is also known as "staying in the moment."

Start every day with meditation, even if it's only for five minutes. It's safe and free, and it will help you focus.

Meditation = focus = success.

# PRAY

The habit of praying is good for you, regardless of whether you believe in God. Prayer achieves the following:

1. **Encourages Gratitude**

   You say thank you for all the good things you have. Being grateful makes you happier.

2. **Helps Others**

   You pray for your loved ones. The exercise of thinking of others promotes unselfishness and triggers your mind to think of ways to help others. If you help others, others will help you.

3. **Stimulates Visualization**

   Everyone prays for help.
   "Please, God, let me pass my exam."
   "Please, God, let me get the deal."
   "Please, God, let that girl fall for me."

   We all want something, and when the chips are down, we close our eyes and pray for it. The act of praying for what you want forces you to visualize your goal and consciously think of the steps required to achieve it. In other words, praying makes you conscious of what you need and how to get it.

   Pray. What do you have to lose?

*You are the average of the five people*
*you spend the most time with.*

— JOHN ROHN —

# 7

## PEOPLE

# FIND YOUR TRIBE

Life without friends is hard, and it's no fun. You have no one to share memories with, no one to celebrate with, and no one to commiserate with.

Finding your tribe is the path to happiness, good memories, and success. On the other hand, hooking up with the wrong people is the path to conflict, angst, and failure. So how do you find your tribe?

First, make sure you avoid the wrong people.

1. **Birds of a Feather Flock Together**

   The best crooks are natural salesmen. They talk a good game. Because penetrating the facade is impossible, look at who he or she hangs out with. Are they your kind of people? Will they make you a better person? If not, take a pass. Birds of a feather flock together—always.

2. **Live a Simple Life**

   A flashy lifestyle attracts the wrong kind of people. Money attracts leeches. Don't stick out for having a fancy car. Keep your life simple, and you'll find that bad people will ignore you.

3. **Ask Your Spouse**

   No one knows you like your spouse. Sometimes he or she can't verbalize why someone is a bad match for you, but when his or her gut is advising you to stay clear, listen to his or her gut. If you're not married yet, get married.

4. **Make Yourself Vulnerable**

   If you want to know whether he or she is going to screw you, make yourself vulnerable. Build in an "engagement" period during which you can break off the relationship easily, and then make it easy for him or her to betray your trust.

## 5. Watch How He or She Treats Other People

Watch how he or she interacts with people when he or she doesn't think you're watching. If he or she treats the cleaner differently from how he or she treats you, stay clear.

## 6. Play Sports

Competitive sport brings out the best—and worst—in people.

Take golf, for example.

Does he or she lose his or her temper if the ball bounces badly? (If so, he or she can't handle adversity.)

Does he or she move his or her ball in the rough? (If so, the person is a cheat.)

Does he or she throw in the towel before the hole is finished? (If so, he or she lacks perseverance.)

Does he or she not care about losing? He or she doesn't care about winning.

Try playing a competitive sport with someone before you bring him or her into your life.

## 7. Turn Up the Temperature

Don't be afraid to crank up the pressure. The only foolproof method for finding out who people really are is to turn up the heat to the point where they crack. You know that you can filter out the wrong people, but how do you find the right people?

Tinder may work for casual sex, but doesn't work for long-term relationships. In general, the best way to find your tribe is to make it easy for them to find you.

How do your people find you?

## 8. Know Thyself

If you don't know who you are, you can't be who you are. If you can't be who you are, you can't be authentic. If you're not authentic, the right people won't be attracted to you. Do everything you can to maximize your self-awareness: find mentors, meditate, travel, read books, take risks, and reflect on your experiences.

Then be yourself.

### 9. Steer Clear of Cliques

Your tribe won't find you unless they know you're looking. Be friendly with everyone. Avoid cliques and mafias. Give everyone the time of day.

### 10. Hold Up a Flag

The right person can't knock on your door if she can't find your door. Make it easy for people to learn about you and your mission. The Internet is the simplest tool for raising a flag. Start a blog, start a vlog, start opening up, and start putting yourself out there. You might think you have nothing of interest to say, but maybe someone else has been waiting his or her whole life to hear what you have to say—and you'll never know unless you try.

Ignore race, religion, language, or age. Your tribe comprises people who share a way of looking at the world, a way of dealing with adversity, and a way of respecting people. They share a way of thinking.

You have to look hard. You have to read a lot. You have to ignore the noise. Just because he or she says the right things doesn't make him or her one of your tribe. Actions speak louder than words, so watch for how people treat other people. Would you do the same?

Find people who resonate with you.

## BE YOURSELF

*It's more powerful if you make a bad first impression*

*and then prove people wrong.*

— MARAIS STEYN —

Don't conform; just be yourself.

Be extremely yourself. You will upset some people, you'll offend others, and you'll even make some enemies. Enemies are inevitable; it's a part of the game and not a big deal. More importantly, in being extremely yourself, you'll attract your tribe.

What's the point of going through life alone? You only get one life; you may as well share it with people who make you happy, who share your world view, and who resonate with you.

Be yourself.

*You have enemies? Good. That means you've stood up*
*for something, sometime in your life.*

— WINSTON CHURCHILL —

# WATCH OUT FOR SLACKERS

*Some cause happiness wherever they go;*
*others whenever they go.*

"Slacker" is the term given for psychopaths, incompetents, and rotten apples who wriggle their way into your life.

The safest way to avoid slackers (and find stars) is to use a checklist before opening the door.

1. Is he or she the type of person who always keeps his or her options open? Avoid people who can't make commitments or stick to their commitments.

2. Who are his or her friends? Birds of a feather flock together.

3. Does he or she use punctuation or paragraphs? Does he or she use too many exclamation marks? In Terry Pratchett's opinion, "Exclamation marks are a sure sign of a diseased mind."

4. Would you introduce him or her to your daughter or son?

5. Does he or she hide behind fancy words? Jargon is the shelter of the incompetent and insecure.

6. Does he or she scan the room with his or her eyes while talking to you?

7. Does he or she badmouth people behind their backs?

8. Does he or she have integrity? Warren Buffett says you should back people with integrity, energy, and intelligence. Without integrity, the others are irrelevant.

9. Are his or her actions, thoughts, and emotions aligned? Does he or she live different lives?

10. Does your gut say that he or she is not "right"? Listen to your gut.

11. Does he or she have the gift of gab? Be doubly careful.

12. Does he or she stand behind his or her opinions, or is he or she always hedging his or her bets?

13. Does he or she make public spectacles of disagreements?

14. Does he or she mimic and kiss the ass of the most powerful person in the room?

15. Is he or she consistent? Consistently friendly or consistently unfriendly are fine; inconsistency is not.

16. Does he or she make excuses and blame others? Is the world out to get him or her? Life is too short to spend time with these people.

17. Does he or she have energy? Stars never need downtime. Slackers always need downtime.

# BEWARE OF PEOPLE WHO KEEP
# THEIR OPTIONS OPEN

*He did nothing in particular and did it very well.*

— W. S. GILBERT —

Some people never commit.

You know the type. Does this sound familiar? You ask him or her whether he or she's in, and his or her response is noncommittal. "Maybe" or "I'll see" or "Check with me closer to time."

These folk can be acquaintances, but they can't be friends for life. True friends must be relied upon. You need to know the person is there and that he or she is committed. When you raise the flag, you can't find the person has deserted his or her post. Go ahead and hang out with footloose and fancy-free people, but don't rely on them. Don't bring them into your life. Friendship requires commitment.

Beware of people who keep their options open.

# DON'T LET FRIENDS
# HOLD YOU BACK

Friendship is like marriage. You must push through the bad times and stay in the kitchen, no matter how hot it gets. Sometimes you've simply chosen the wrong person. Maybe he or she's into drugs, maybe he or she's dishonest, or maybe he or she's not ambitious. Whatever it is, he or she isn't making you a better person. Don't persevere. Cut him or her loose. Spend time with people who make you a better person.

Friendship should last a lifetime, but life is too short to be stuck in a relationship that's holding you back.

*Spend your time with happy people.*

— ANET PIENAAR —

## DON'T LET PEOPLE UPSET YOU

The world needs asses and crooks and liars.

Everyone has a role, even if that role is only to make you look good.

Stay clear of the wrong kind of people. Find your own tribe. Choose your friends carefully. Don't let baddies work you into a froth. Walk a mile in their shoes, and you'd probably be the same person. It's better to simply take note of who's an ass, and stay clear in future. If someone has a problem with you, that's his or her problem, not yours.

# STAY AWAY FROM
# ENERGY VAMPIRES

*I never forget a face, but in your case
I'll be glad to make an exception.*

— Groucho Marx —

Some people suck your energy; you know who I'm talking about. Maybe they're pessimistic. Maybe they're lazy. Maybe they're boring. Maybe they're just plain asses. They suck your energy. You feel time slow down when you're with them. You dread seeing them. They're not evil; they're just energy vampires.

Energy is the most valuable thing you have, more so than money or time. Do not waste it, and do not let it be drained. Stay away from people who take your energy. Find people who give you energy. Hang out with people you look forward to seeing. Spend time with people who make time go fast. These are the people who help you move forward in life, so you should stick with them.

Stay away from energy vampires.

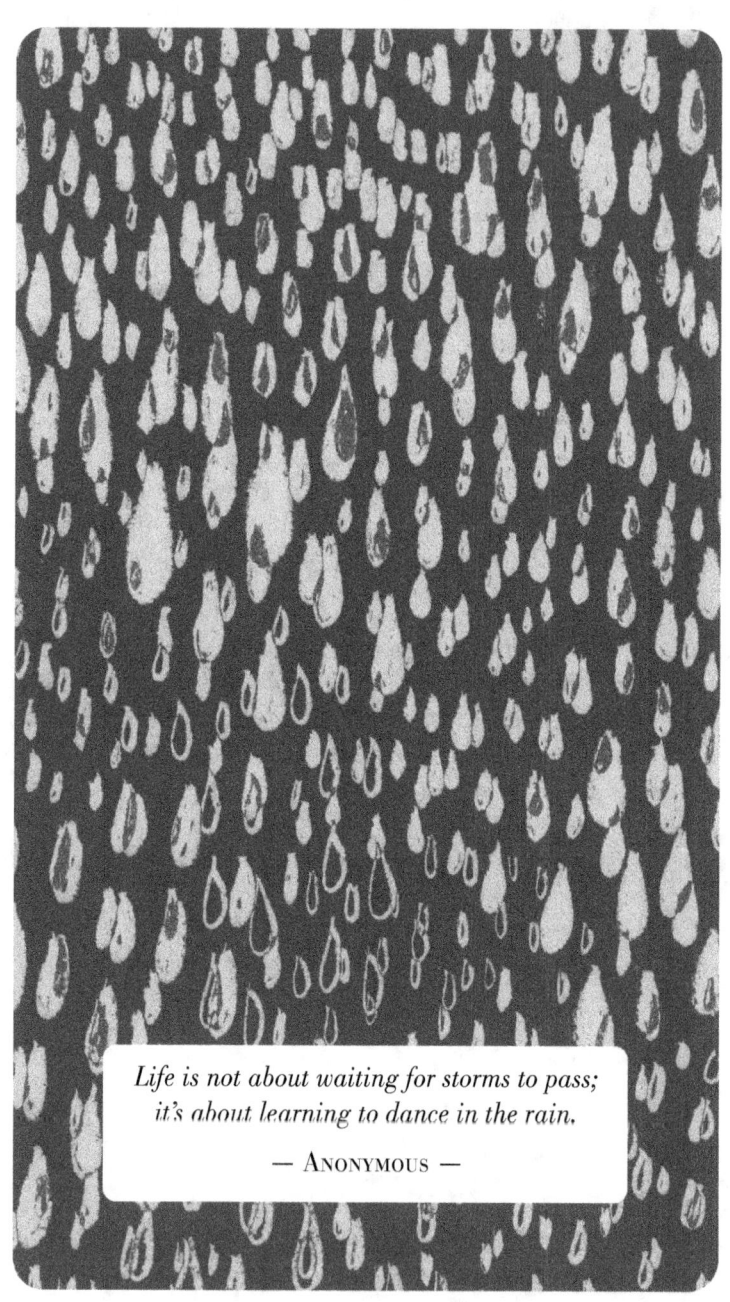

*Life is not about waiting for storms to pass;*
*it's about learning to dance in the rain.*

— Anonymous —

# 8

## ADVERSITY

# DEFEAT IS OKAY

Extract from the manuscripts of Accra:

Defeat means that we lose a particular battle or war. Failure does not allow us to go on fighting.

Defeat comes when we fail to get something we very much want. Failure does not allow us to dream. Its motto is "Expect nothing, and you won't be disappointed."

Defeat ends when we launch into another battle. Failure has no end: it is a lifetime choice.

Defeat is for those who, despite their fears, live with enthusiasm and faith.

Defeat is for the valiant. Only they will know the honour of losing and the joy of winning.

Only the defeated know love. Because it is in the realm of love that we fight our first battles—and generally lose. There are people who have never been defeated. They are the ones who never fought. They managed to avoid scars, humiliations, and feelings of helplessness, as well as those moments when even warriors doubt the existence of God. Such people can say with pride, "I never lost a battle." On the other hand, they will never be able to say: "I won a battle."

Not that they care. They live in a universe in which they believe they are invulnerable, they close their eyes to injustices and to suffering; they feel safe because they do not have to deal with the daily challenges faced by those who risk stepping out beyond their own boundaries.

They have never heard the words "good-bye" or "I've come back. Embrace me with the fervour of someone who, having lost me, has found me again."

Those who were never defeated seem happy and superior,

masters of a truth they never had to lift a finger to achieve. They are always on the side of the strong. They're like hyenas, who only eat the leavings of lions.

They teach their children: "Don't get involved in conflicts, you'll only lose. Keep your doubts to yourself and you'll never have any problems. If someone attacks you, don't get offended or demean yourself by hitting back. There are more important things in life."

In the silence of the night, they fight their imaginary battles: their unrealized dreams, the injustices to which they turned a blind eye, the moments of cowardice they managed to conceal from people—but not from themselves—and the love that crossed their path with a sparkle in its eyes, the love God had intended for them, but which they lacked the courage to embrace.

And they promise themselves that "Tomorrow will be different."

But tomorrow comes and the paralysing question surfaces in their mind: "What if it doesn't work out?"

And so they do nothing.

Woe to those who were never beaten! They will never be winners in this life.


## STOP WAITING FOR
## SOMEONE TO SAVE YOU

Feeling sorry for yourself?

Stop.

Feel the world owes you something?

Stop.

Waiting for someone to save you?

Stop.

No one will save you. The world owes you nothing. Don't feel sorry for yourself. Don't be a victim. Take control of your life. Wake up early. Choose your friends wisely. Start moving forward. Stop waiting for opportunity to knock on your door. Go out and grab opportunity. Do not wait to strike till the iron is hot. Make it hot by striking.


## DON'T BE A VICTIM

A victim mentality is a cage. It traps you, and it renders you powerless when things don't go your way.

"Why me?"

"Life is so unfair."

"I don't deserve this."

Life is unfair. No one deserves anything. Sometimes bad things happen to good people. Accept it, get on with life, and keep moving.

# DON'T BLAME OTHER PEOPLE

Life is mostly random.

Bad stuff happens. Sometimes setbacks are a direct result of a mistake, but most times, it's just bad luck. Either way, you can't blame yourself or others. Blaming gets you stuck. It dissipates energy and stops you from moving forward.

When things don't go your way, take a moment to reflect on whether you could have done anything differently. Add the lesson to your notebook.

Forget it and move on.

If you can't find any reasons for your setback, don't panic. The universe is infinite, and there are more moving parts than you can comprehend. Sometimes you're just in the way of an oncoming truck—and boom! Accidents happen. Keep moving.

*In my experience, men who respond to good fortune with modesty and kindness are harder to find than those who face adversity with courage.*

— CYRUS THE GREAT —

# TACKLE OBSTACLES HEAD ON

In a jam? There's only one thing you can do: keep moving forward.

When things don't go your way, your instincts will tell you to freeze. "Don't move! Play dead! Eventually the bad stuff will lose interest and disappear!" Your instincts are wrong; you can't pretend your problems away.

Amelia Earhart, the famous pilot, had a sticker on her plane that read "Always think with your stick forward." In other words, no matter the dilemma, keep flying.

You have to take your challenges head on. If you can't go around or over the obstacle, go through the obstacle. No matter what, keep moving. The best way to move is at top speed. Overwhelm through energy. Press, press, press until you find the chink in the wall and then, boom! Break through the wall.

What's the alternative? Stay where you are? Find the easy path? Good luck with that. The hard path is where the opportunity lies. The obstacles exist for your competitors too. No one said it would be easy, so put your head down and concentrate.

There's only one way out, and that's flat out.

# DON'T RUN AWAY

Sometimes you hit a wall.

Your instincts kick in. Fight or flight?

If you're sane, your brain says, "Run!"

Your husband or wife says, "Run!"

Your parents say, "Run!"

Run away from the blast zone. "Save yourself!" Maybe that's the smart thing to do, but that's not what a hero does. A hero gets up and fights. You will encounter some seriously unpleasant patches when you decide to follow your dreams. You have to suck it up and take the good with the bad.

Running away doesn't solve your problems; it simply delays the inevitable. When you're finally forced to confront reality, the explosion is much bigger.

Tackle your fears early. Don't run away.

# FORGET ABOUT REVENGE

*The weak can never forgive.*
*Forgiveness is the attribute of the strong.*

— Mahatma Gandhi —

So you've been screwed. So you've been betrayed. So you've been beaten.

So what?

Justice is not your job; leave it to karma. What goes around will come around. Your job is to be a success. Success lies with what can be taken from the future, not what can be reclaimed from the past.

Let it go.

Reflect, learn lessons, and move on. Revenge is a negative motive, and it generates negative energy. Only negative things can come of it. Stay in the light.

*Revenge is an admission of pain;*
*a mind that is bowed by injury is not a great mind.*

— Seneca —

# TAKE IT ON THE CHIN

*Harden up. Life is rough and tumble.*

— DENIS O'BRIEN —

Sometimes you'll lose money, your lover will cheat on you, your friend will betray you... or whatever.

That's just how it goes. Being an entrepreneur means taking risks, and risks mean accepting the chance of failure. When things don't go your way, be cool. Don't rant and rave and blame the world. Dry your eyes. Suck it up. Take responsibility. Take it on the chin.

If you can't take setbacks on the chin, you can't be an entrepreneur.

# FOUR STEPS FOR RECOVERING FROM FAILURE

You might have a huge setback in life. Whatever you do, don't make any rash decisions. Life is like love: rebound relationships usually end in tears. If you can afford to, force yourself to take six months off before deciding on the way forward. During the break, do the following.

1. **Read Necessary Endings, by Dr. Henry Cloud**

   Read it because this is an essential reading for anyone going through a big change in life, for example, divorce, changing career, and so on.

2. **Clear Your Head**

Get out of Dodge. Get away from the noise. Pack your family into a car and take a road trip. Better yet, fly to a time zone on the other side of the world where no one knows you or can call you. Give yourself space and time to process your thoughts and deal with the emotions of failure.

## 3. Reassess Your Priorities

Did you keep your family first? Did you enjoy what you were doing? Are you living in the right town? The right country? Starting over again is the ideal moment for making the pivotal decisions needed to realign your career with your life. Choose the town you want to live in, choose a business model that won't compromise your family life, and then do what you love.

## 4. Reflect on Your Lessons

Big setbacks are the richest learning opportunities you'll ever have. You'll learn about yourself, about life, and about other people. Sit down and write what you've learnt. What are your strengths? What are your weaknesses? What would you do differently? Make a list of all the people who stood by you, as well as the ones who suddenly lost your phone number. One day you'll be on top of the wheel. That is a great place to be, but it doesn't teach you much.

Learn your lessons when you hit the ground.

# THERE'S ONLY ONE WAY
# OUT OF A JAM

Feeling stressed? Back against the wall? Running out of cash? Running out of time? In a jam? There's only one way out: flat out.

When your back is against the wall, you have a choice. Will you wait for them to finish you off—or will you come out fighting?

Choose the latter. Double down on effort. Shout out from the rooftops. Act crazy. Go in arms flailing. Take every inch of energy you have and invest it in getting what you want.

When you're in a jam, there's only one way out: flat out.

# SOMETIMES YOU HAVE TO
# PLAY DEAD

Most times, the best way to deal with a problem is to tackle it head on. Show no fear.

Sometimes the problem is better left alone, especially in the case of people. Some people gain energy from you engaging directly. No matter how good your case is, your attention is a form of validation that only makes them stronger. At times like these, the best strategy is to "play dead." Don't take calls, don't reply to e-mails, and don't resort to insults. Even the most persistent of naggers will eventually wander off to find more fun fights.

Conserve your energy for where it's needed most.

Play dead.

# SEVEN TRICKS FOR
# FIGHTING FEAR

Only fools don't feel fear. There's no escaping it. All you can do is try to manage it. Here are some tricks to keep fear in check.

1. **Meditate:** Clearing your mind is a powerful way to quiet the little voice in your head and remove your doubts.

2. **Prepare:** "Don't take a knife to a gunfight." Preparation will give you confidence.

3. **Imagine the worst scenario:** The real-life consequences of losing are rarely as bad as your imagination makes them out to be. Think it through, and you'll be less scared.

4. **Cultivate close relationships:** The more social ties you have, the braver you will be.

5. **Act brave:** Psychologist William James proved that if you act confident, your body will produce the hormones that make you confident. Outward appearances can impact your mental state. Stand tall with your shoulders back.

6. **Read:** The more you read, the more you'll realize you're not alone. Many others have been in worse situations and survived. Why won't you?

7. **Fail:** The more you take risks, fail, and survive, the more you will overcome the fear of failure.

# THIS TOO SHALL PASS

There are times in life when you feel overwhelmed—bickering staff, bad press, no parking. The temptation is to step in, get involved, solve the problem, and get things under control—but you should resist the temptation.

Most things will resolve themselves. Most problems are just noise. Ignore the noise. Weather the storm. "This too shall pass" applies to most things. Meddling in the small stuff will usually make matters worse. The important stuff is cash flow and coffee. Focus on family, cash flow, and coffee.

As for the rest, be cool.

*Adversity makes men, and prosperity makes monsters.*

— VICTOR HUGO —

# 9

# LEARNING

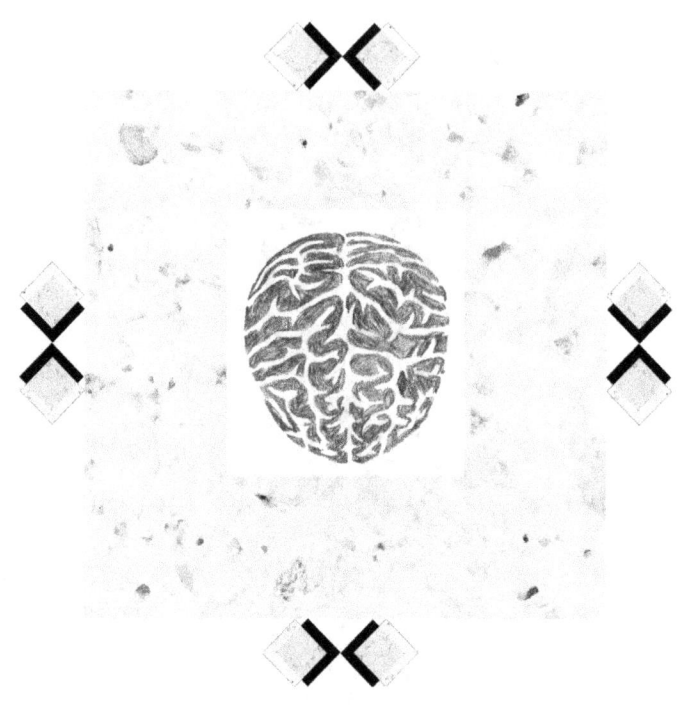

*You don't want to learn too many lessons,*
*otherwise you won't take any risks.*

— THEO RUTSTEIN —

# TELL YOUR STORY

If a tree falls in a forest and no one is there to hear it, did it make a sound?

Most rational people say, "Yes, of course it made a sound. A lack of witnesses does not negate the reality of a tree making a sound when it falls over." That's why most rational people never get anywhere in life. The right answer is, "No. The tree did not make a sound if no one heard it."

Grasping this fundamental truth is key to taking responsibility for your life, career, and dreams. "Build it, and they will come" is a mantra for losers. The world is busy. People are being bombarded by information all day every day, and the mobile Web is only making the fire hose bigger. People don't have time to find you; you need to get their attention. Otherwise, you'll go through life thinking, I'm so awesome, but no one gives me credit. Oh, woe is me.

Opportunity can't knock on your door if you don't have a door or if no one can find your house. You have to put yourself out there and risk making a fool of yourself. The tree only makes a sound if there's a witness.

# SEVEN TIPS TO IMPROVE
# YOUR MEMORY

1. If you don't tell yourself you have a great memory, you'll never have a great memory. Pretend your memory is great.

2. Your brain stores memories using all five senses. The more of them you use, the more likely you are to remember. Keep a diary (physical sensation of writing). Use a pencil (to hear yourself writing). Use scented paper (to smell the writing).

3. Associate names with images.

4. Repetition, repetition, repetition: say it enough, and it will stick.

5. Practice. Instead of looking up your flight reservation number at the check-in desk, memorize it (it's only six characters). Get into the habit of exercising your memory muscle.

6. Build yourself a memory palace. Don't know what that is? Google it.

7. Live an exciting life. If every day is like the day before, you'll never remember a single day. Excitement equals risk. Take risks, and you'll find your memory improves.

# SIX RULES FOR WRITING

BY GEORGE ORWELL

1.  Never use a metaphor, simile, or other figure of speech which you are used to seeing in print.

2.  Never use a long word where a short one will do.

3.  If it is possible to cut a word out, always cut it out.

4.  Never use the passive where you can use the active.

5.  Never use a foreign phrase, a scientific word, or a jargon word if you can think of an everyday English equivalent.

6.  Break any of these rules sooner than say anything outright barbarous.

# THE DIFFERENCE BETWEEN THINKERS AND DOERS

*Only the guy who isn't rowing has time to rock the boat.*

— JEAN-PAUL SARTRE —

There are two extremes in life that you want to avoid: extreme thinkers and extreme doers.

An extreme thinker is like a guy who is so busy planning his urination that he forgets to unzip. Instead, he wets his pants. The satisfaction of having designed the perfect wee is spoilt by the realization that his wardrobe must now be replaced.

An extreme doer is like a guy who is so intent on getting the job done that instead of thinking things through, he wees on his hands (and pants and sometimes his shirt). The warming sensation on his hands gives the misguided perception of progress, whereas in fact, he is making more work for himself.

Keep a safe distance from extreme thinkers—and be careful of shaking hands with extreme doers.

# TWENTY-THREE TIPS FOR BECOMING A BETTER NEGOTIATOR

1. First impressions count. Dress smart and smile.

2. Home games are preferable. Your office is a stronger base to negotiate from.

3. Expect to be liked. The other person will notice. Likability is key to doing deals.

4. Make small talk. Don't charge into the details. Create a comfortable atmosphere.

5. Be positive. Be optimistic.

6. Be nice.

7. Mimic. Copy the other person's body language and words.

8. Look for commonality. Common ground is the best place from which to start.

9. Get three consecutive yeses, and you'll get the deal.

10. Be humble; no one likes arrogance.

11. Flattery will get you everywhere.

12. Listen.

13. Say "we."

14. Act stupid when you're smart.

15. Act smart when you're stupid.

16. Body language is important. Don't fold your arms.

17. Be confident. Act confident.

18. Ninety-nine cents is better than one dollar.

19. Don't use round numbers.

20. Sometimes it's best to be the first to put a number on the table.

21. No evidence is better than weak evidence.

22. Repetition, repetition, repetition.

23. Have a good time. Life is short.

# THE ART OF SELLING

An entrepreneur must know how to persuade people, how to win arguments, and how to sell.

You can't get ahead without learning how to sell. You need to be a salesman. Selling is an art, a learnt skill. Some people are born with the gift of gab, but the best salesmen are those for whom it doesn't come naturally. Why? Because when customers can see you're not comfortable selling, they trust that you wouldn't be standing there sweating unless you truly believed in what you're pushing.

The first big sell you have in life is your spouse. You need to convince someone who's out of your league that you are, in fact, worthy.

Here are some tips:

### 1. Tell the Truth

Always tell the truth. Lying is a short-term strategy. It may work in a big country like the United States, where you can move around a lot, but in South Africa, if you get divorced, you're still brother and sister.

With the arrival of social media, our small town is getting smaller every day. If you lie, you'll be found out, and then it's tickets for your career as a salesman.

Tell the truth. That way, you don't have to remember what you said.

## 2. Listen to the Customer

Most people think selling is about talking. Wrong—selling is about listening. You can't give the customer what he or she wants unless you know what he or she wants. If the customer wants hot dogs, don't sell him or her hamburgers.

## 3. Make a Good First Impression

First impressions may not be everything, but it's much easier getting a yes if you make a positive first impression. Be neat. Be on time. Be prepared. Be polite.

Don't fake it. If you're not a suit wearer, don't wear a suit. If the girl of your dreams loves guys in suits, chase another girl. Pretending to be someone you're not is akin to lying. It's a short-term strategy doomed to failure, and that's not a great way to live.

## 4. Help People

The more you help people, the more people will help you. What goes around comes around.

## 5. Show Respect

It's very simple, and yet, so many people don't do it. Take the time to learn the culture of your customer. For example, did you know Tswana consider it a sign of disrespect to make eye contact when shaking hands?

Have good manners, respect local customs, and be patient. No one will say yes if they feel you don't respect them.

## 6. Do Whatever Has to Be Done

Sometimes you have to suck up your ego and wait outside his

or her window for hours. Sometimes you have to dress up to go to a dance party. Sometimes you have to dance! You have to do whatever needs to be done to win him or her over. No one else will do it.

7. **Close the Deal**

It's easy to mess around and avoid the hard questions like, "Will you marry me?"

Some people specialize in messing others around. The best way to find out whether you're being messed around is to ask for a commitment. Maybe means no.

For a master class in how to sell, read Mark McCormack's What They Don't Teach You at Harvard Business School and Harry Beckwith's Selling the Invisible.

If you're not ready to be a salesman, you're not ready to be an entrepreneur.

# CHANGE YOUR MIND

*When the facts change, I change my mind.*
*What do you do?*

— JOHN MAYNARD KEYNES —

You should cringe at some of the things you've said in the past.

If you're not cringing, you're not growing. As you go through life and experience new things, your perspective changes. You learn stuff. You grow up. In life, you'll sometimes be forced to take a view, defend a position, and be opinionated. You'll say some stupid things; it's inevitable.

The trick is to accept that you'll make mistakes. When you realize you said or did something stupid, acknowledge it, course correct, and move on. Everyone—as well-meaning and learned as they seem—makes mistakes. Making mistakes doesn't matter. The only thing that matters is that you are honest with yourself and have the guts to admit it.

If it's your life, it's your mistake. If you fail, you can't point fingers and say, "But he said…" It doesn't matter if people think you're a fool. You can't build a life based on other people's opinions. At the end of the day, your life is your responsibility. If you want to succeed, you must keep learning. The only way you learn is if you admit your mistakes and change your mind.

*Learn as if you were going to live forever.*
*Live as if you were to die tomorrow.*

— MAHATMA GANDHI —

# 10

## FAMILY

# DON'T NEGLECT YOUR FAMILY

For most people, life is not a rose garden. Life is a war—a war for recognition, a war for success, or a war for survival. When you're at war, family is the most important thing there is. Without it, you'll find yourself standing in the middle of a big green field with thousands of bullets and missiles and drones racing at you.

You'll be alone if you don't have family. Your family—your parents, your kids, and most importantly, your spouse—are your core.

Don't neglect your family.

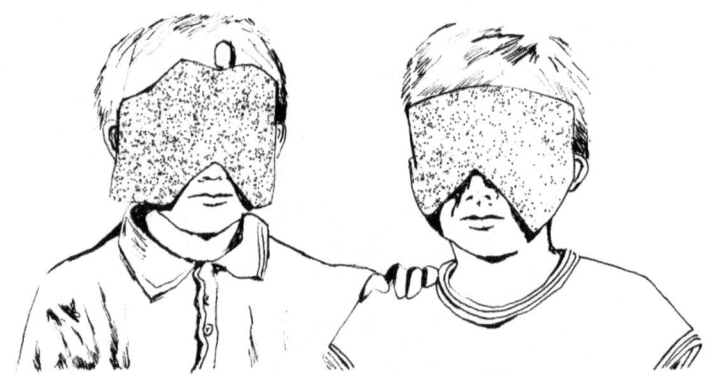

# SEVEN REASONS TO MARRY YOUNG

*By all means marry; if you get a good wife, you'll become happy; if you get a bad one, you'll become a philosopher.*

— SOCRATES —

1. **Fewer Distractions**

   When you're single, you spend a lot of time worrying, texting, dating, and hunting. Marriage cancels this noise, freeing up time and energy to chase your dreams.

2. **Financial Security**

   A dual income in a single household means more disposable income every month.

3. **Emotional Support**

   Sometimes you're on a winning streak, and your ego needs a check. Sometimes setbacks are hitting you left and right, and you need a loving shoulder. Your spouse will pull you back down to earth when you get carried away and pick you up when you fall.

4. **Marry before You Make Money**

   It's best to find your spouse before your career takes off. That way, you can be sure she or he married you for you, not for your money.

5. **Fewer Hangovers, More Sleep**

   When you're single, you're socializing. That means alcohol, parties, and late nights. When you're married, the incentive to go out is reduced, leaving you better rested and able to concentrate on getting ahead in life.

### 6. Marriage Is Extremely Fun without Kids

You want to have some years of marriage without kids, simply because it's so much fun! That means marrying young, because when you turn thirty, the babies start arriving.

### 7. Mutual Admiration Society

No one likes a braggart. A spouse can sing your praises without you seeming insufferably arrogant. All you need to do is support and praise your partner, and voila! You'll have happiness and success.

A bonus reason to marry young is just in case you marry the wrong person. You can then divorce young and try again. Fail fast.

# SEVEN WAYS CHILDREN
# MAKE YOU A BETTER PERSON

*I believe that children are our future.*
*Unless we stop them now.*

— HOMER SIMPSON —

1. **Children teach perseverance.** You will spend many a night walking in darkness, cradling an infant with his eyes wide open, toying with the idea of infanticide and close to the precipice of giving up. The only thing that will keep you going is the fact that no one else will do the job. You can't give up. The same applies to life. You can't outsource your life. You can't quit.

2. **Children make you swear less.**

3. **Children keep you in the moment.**

4. **Children make you behave as a role model.** Imagining your kid reading about you in the Sunday papers is a great incentive for always doing the right thing.

5. **Children make you spend more time at home.**

6. **Children give you a deeper purpose than just making money.**

7. **Children don't care when you fail.** To them, you're always Mom or Dad, and you can never fail. You're awesome.

# The Little Chap Who Follows Me

*A careful man I want to be;*
*A little fellow follows me.*
*I do not dare to go astray*
*For fear he'll go the self-same way.*

*I cannot once escape his eyes,*
*Whate'er he sees me do, he tries.*
*Like me he says he's going to be;*
*The little chap who follows me.*

*He thinks that I'm so very fine,*
*Believes in every word of mine.*
*The base in me he must not see;*
*The little chap who follows me.*

*I must remember as I go*
*Through summer's sun and winter's snow,*
*I'm building for the years to be;*
*The little chap who follows me.*

AUTHOR: UNKNOWN

## MAKE A LIVING AND LIVE
## AT THE SAME TIME

Some people think that work and life are separate worlds, never to be mixed.

You go to work to make money so that you can spend that money to live.

Entrepreneurs can't afford to do that. Life is too short to delay your dreams. You must ensure your work is living; otherwise, you may never have a chance to live.

What is living? Living is having fun, making memories, meeting people, and generally learning all the time while doing what you love. Love what you do and turn every day into a learning experience. Like sucking the last puff from a cigarette butt, you should drag the most out of every moment, good and bad. Make sure you're living while making a living.

# BE PRESENT

You get home after a long day, and your parents, your kids, or your spouse welcome you home. They start telling you about their day, and already your mind is wandering to that e-mail you haven't sent, that call you haven't made, or that boy or girl you're trying to date. You decide to sneak in a few quick messages on your phone. It's important the world knows that you're alive.

Stop it!

The world doesn't matter. The only thing that matters is being 100 percent present in whatever you do. Family is the most important thing for you. Switch off your phone when you get home. If you have work to do, wake up at 5:00 a.m. If you have lots of work, wake up at 4:00 a.m. If you can be 100 percent present, your relationship with your parents, your kids, and your spouse will improve. The better your relationship with your family, the greater your odds of success.

There is a background hum of nervous mental energy that increasingly pervades our daily lives. To reduce the hum, minimize distractions. Switch off your phone.

# TEACH YOUR CHILDREN

*Listen to your children when they want to speak,*
*not when you want to listen.*

— ERROL KRUGER —

We all want our children to be okay in life. We want them to find jobs, get married, and be happy and healthy.

The problem is that the world's advice for helping your child find success is to go to school, get A's, go to a top university, get top marks, get a great job, get a mortgage, etc.

All of the above is wrong: School is not important; university is not important; a job is definitely not important. The world is changing. Twenty years from now, the most valuable opportunities in the world will be for those people who understand how to solve problems. The first step in solving problems is not to panic when confronted with a challenge. You need to tackle the problem without the fear of failure. If you fail in your first attempt, you need to keep trying. No one else will help you with your problem.

School doesn't teach you this. School teaches you that the world is ordered and predictable and that if you memorize your homework, you can get an A in your test. School teaches you that failing is bad. School teaches you that being friends with the cool kids is crucial to success. School is important, but it won't prepare your child for the real world. Only you can do that.

The good news is there's help at hand. Video games alone are teaching children more about problem solving and failure than most parents could on their own. All you need to do is give your kids your undivided attention for a couple of hours every day. Give your kids the love of reading. Give your kids access to the

Internet. If you raise them properly, they'll enter the real world able to confront uncertainty and solve their own problems.

It's your responsibility to teach them. No one else will.

# THE SIX-MONTH RULE

Had enough? Ready to quit? Want to find another spouse? Considering leaving the country?

Wait six months. If you feel the same in six months, then pull the trigger. If not, don't do anything. When it comes to big decisions, it's best to wait to see if "this too shall pass." While you wait, give 100 percent effort to make sure you're not making a mistake. Give it your all for another six months, and then make the call.

# COURAGE

*Courage is the finest of all human qualities*

*because it guarantees the others.*

— Winston Churchill —

## GO INTO THE LION'S DEN

Do whatever makes your afraid.

Scared to speak in front of a crowd? Do it.

Scared to speak to your bank manager? Do it.

Scared to break up with your boyfriend or girlfriend? Do it.

Scared to tell your parents you want to be an artist? Do it.

Procrastinating slows you down. If you slow down, you'll fail. Suck it up, confront whatever makes you afraid. Go into the lion's den.

# THE MAN IN THE ARENA

Excerpt from the speech "Citizenship in a Republic" delivered at the Sorbonne, in Paris, France, on April 23, 1910, by Franklin Roosevelt.

It is not the critic who counts; not the man who points out how the strong man stumbles, or where the doer of deeds could have done them better. The credit belongs to the man who is actually in the arena, whose face is marred by dust and sweat and blood; who strives valiantly; who errs, who comes short again and again, because there is no effort without error and shortcoming; but who does actually strive to do the deeds; who knows great enthusiasms, the great devotions; who spends himself in a worthy cause; who at the best knows in the end the triumph of high achievement, and who at the worst, if he fails, at least fails while daring greatly, so that his place shall never be with those cold and timid souls who neither know victory nor defeat.

# THE COURAGE TO COPY COWARDS

It takes guts to be an entrepreneur. You must overcome the fear of failure, the fear of embarrassment, and the fear of pain. You don't need courage if you don't feel fear. The fearless are not worthy of copying; they have no courage. Rather, copy the cowards who have overcome their cowardice.

# THE COURAGE TO FOLLOW

It's easy to go your own way. It's a lot harder to throw your lot in with someone else. Sometimes you need the guts to get on someone else's ship and trust they won't drive you straight into an iceberg.

# THE COURAGE TO FIGHT

*If a person is intelligent, then of course, he is a coward.*
*This is an automatic definition of high intelligence.*

— JOHN FOWLES —

Fighting with fists or with lawyers is not for sissies. It takes guts to get into a fight, especially when you know you're outmatched. Entrepreneurs have guts.

# THE COURAGE TO LEAD

It's easy to go it on your own and reject responsibility for a team. It's a lot harder to take the mantle of a leader and show your followers the way.

# THE COURAGE TO SPEAK UP

It's easy to nod, say yes, and go with the crowd. It takes guts to speak the truth, especially when you're speaking to power.

# THE COURAGE TO CARRY ON

*Many of life's failures are people*
*who did not realize how close they were to success*
*when they gave up.*

— THOMAS EDISON —

Every successful person in the world will give this answer for how they made it in life: persevere. Have the guts to push on, even when it seems the end is nigh.

# THE COURAGE TO QUIT

*Failure is unimportant.*
*It takes courage to make a fool of yourself.*

— CHARLIE CHAPLIN —

Sometimes it's harder to quit than to persevere.

Peer pressure, sunk costs in effort and money, and your reputation—what will people think? Throwing in the towel means confronting so many ugly truths that you instead choose the easy path: Carry on. Be a zombie, the living dead. Being a zombie doesn't help anyone.

People make mistakes. If you chose the wrong path, turn around and go back to the fork in the road. Try again. Have the courage to say, "I made a mistake."

# THE COURAGE TO IGNORE
# THE CROWD

*We set our course by the stars,*
*not by the lights of every passing ship.*

— OMAR N. BRADLEY —

Conformists are cowards. They don't have the guts to fight the crowd. They know they are defeated before they start. They meekly get into line and follow instructions, even though they know the path is wrong.

Don't be that person.

Maybe you can't speak out. Maybe you can't intervene. Maybe you can't stop the crowd, but you don't have to follow. When you have power, have the guts to get off the sidelines. When you know something is wrong, have the guts to speak out. When the crowd goes off in the wrong direction, have the guts to stay behind.

## THE COURAGE TO FACE THE TRUTH

Do you avoid getting to the bottom of things?

Maybe you fear being impolite.

Maybe you fear hurting yourself.

Maybe you fear hurting others.

Whatever the reason, it's always fear. That fear means you can't be a success. There is no safety net for you, no hiding from the facts. No one is bailing you out. Only you can bail yourself out. To save yourself, you need to know what's going on.

Ask the hard questions, and dig for the answers; the truth will set you free.

# THE COURAGE TO FACE
# THE FEAR OF FAILURE

The fear of failure is a great motivator. In the darkest hours, you need more than just the promise of a pot of gold to get you out of bed. Fear gets you out of bed. The fear of losing your house, your reputation, or your family gets you out of bed.

The danger of fear of failure (or fear of anything) is in letting it overwhelm you. That causes panic, overreaction, or emotions that suppress rational thought. You make the wrong decisions, and the fear becomes self-fulfilling. If you can maintain perspective, you'll realize how small your problems are in the grand scheme of things and how insignificant your life is in the universe.

Read stoic philosophy, and don't be afraid of fear. Welcome it. After all, it gets you out of bed.

*Success is not final. Failure is not fatal.*
*It is the courage to continue that counts.*

— Winston Churchill —

**IF,** by Rudyard Kipling

*If you can keep your head when all about you*
*Are losing theirs and blaming it on you;*
*If you can trust yourself when all men doubt you,*
*But make allowance for their doubting too;*
*If you can wait and not be tired by waiting,*
*Or being lied about, don't deal in lies,*
*Or being hated, don't give way to hating,*
*And yet don't look too good, nor talk too wise:*

*If you can dream—and not make dreams your master;*
*If you can think—and not make thoughts your aim;*
*If you can meet with Triumph and Disaster*
*And treat those two imposters just the same;*
*If you can bear to hear the truth you've spoken*
*Twisted by knaves to make a trap for fools,*
*Or watch the things you gave your life to, broken,*
*And stoop and build 'em up with worn-out tools;*

*If you can make one heap of all your winnings*
*And risk it on one turn of pitch-and-toss,*
*And lose, and start again at your beginnings*
*And never breathe a word about your loss;*
*If you can force your heart and nerve and sinew*
*To serve your turn long after they are gone,*
*And so hold on when there is nothing in you*
*Except the Will which says to them: "Hold on!"*

*If you can talk with crowds and keep your virtue,*
*Or walk with kings—nor lose the common touch,*
*If neither foes nor loving friends can hurt you,*
*If all men count with you, but none too much;*
*If you can fill the unforgiving minute*
*With sixty seconds' worth of distance run—*
*Yours is the Earth and everything that's in it,*
*And—which is more—you'll be a Man, my son!*

# 12

## PEARLS OF WISDOM

# THE PURPOSE-DRIVEN LIFE

BY RICK WARREN

Don't associate with people you can't trust.
Don't cheat. Don't lie. Don't pretend.
Don't dictate because you are smarter.
Don't demand because you are stronger.

Don't date because you are desperate.
Don't marry because you are miserable.
Don't have kids because you think your genes are superior.
Don't philander because you think you are irresistible.

Don't sleep around because you think you are old enough and know better.
Don't hurt your kids because loving them is harder.
Don't sell yourself, your family, or your ideals.
Don't stagnate!

Don't regress.
Don't live in the past. Time can't bring anything or anyone back.
Don't put your life on hold for possibly Mr./Mrs. Right.
Don't throw your life away on absolutely Mr./Mrs. Wrong because your biological clock is ticking.

Learn a new skill.
Find a new friend.
Start a new career.
Sometimes, there is no race to be won, only a price to be paid for some of life's more hasty decisions.
To terminate your loneliness, reach out to the homeless.
To feed your nurturing instincts, care for the needy.
To fulfil your parenting fantasies, get a puppy.
Don't bring another life into this world for all the wrong reasons.
To make yourself happy, pursue your passions and be the best of

what you can be.

Simplify your life. Take away the clutter.
Get rid of destructive elements: abusive friends, nasty habits, and dangerous liaisons.
Don't abandon your responsibilities but don't overdose on duty.

Don't live life recklessly without thought and feeling for your family.
Be true to yourself.
Don't commit when you are not ready.
Don't keep others waiting needlessly.

Go on that trip. Don't postpone it. Say those words. Don't let the moment pass.
Do what you have to, even at society's scorn.

Write poetry. Love deeply.
Walk barefoot. Dance with wild abandon. Cry at the movies.

Take care of yourself. Don't wait for someone to take care of you.
You light up your life. You drive yourself to your destination. No one completes you—except you.

It isn't true that life does not get easier with age.
It only gets more challenging.
Don't be afraid. Don't lose your capacity to love.
Pursue your passions.

Live your dreams. Don't lose faith in God. Don't grow old. Just grow you!

# LEADERSHIP, DPJ STYLE

*Derek Prout-Jones is the former chief
investment officer of Rand Merchant Bank.*

1. **Always Lead from the Front**

   That doesn't necessarily mean leading the charge and winning
   a posthumous VC like Col "H" Jones in the Falklands (and
   leaving your battalion without a leader); but it does mean
   setting the right example for your team to follow. Arriving at
   work late and leaving early on a regular basis while expecting
   your people to put in long hours is not conducive to garnering
   their respect. It also means never giving someone a task that
   you wouldn't (n.b., not couldn't) do yourself.

2. **Surround Yourself with the Best Possible People**

   A weak manager will choose a mediocre team so as not to be
   threatened. Successful leaders absolutely require a quality
   team with diverse and complementary skills; and people who
   are prepared to stand up to him/her to defend their point of
   view.

3. **Use Collective Wisdom**

   Almost always we > me. Seek your team's advice and input.
   This will make them feel part of the solution and builds esprit
   des corps. Of course, this goes hand in hand with 2 above.

4. **Be a Good Listener**

   Many managers are only interested in talking. You will learn
   more from listening than talking. You need this quality to get
   the most from 3 above.

5. **Be Courageous**

   Have the guts to make those hard calls that we all hate to
   make. When appropriate, be prepared to pull a "Col H. Jones"

on yourself and take a bullet for the team. It also means being bold enough to drive change where it is required and (even) admitting when you are wrong.

6. **Set a Clear Strategy**
Make sure the team knows what the mission is and what the target is. Getting the team's input in the process is vital to ensure buy-in (as in 3 above). Then give them the freedom to execute and achieve it. "Power is more about how many people you liberate than how many you control!" Do not keep your team in the dark!

7. **Be Prepared to Reward Superperformance**
This may mean paying a subordinate more than you for excellent work. Sounds easy, but is not in practice.

8. **Always Be Seen as Being Fair**
Treat people equitably. Never show favoritism.

9. **Know When to Leave**
There comes a time in every leader's life to step aside for the good of the business and those around you. Better to leave too early than too late.

## GUARDING YOUR PASSION

BY LYNETTE FINLAY

*Lynette Finlay is the founder of Finlay Properties.*

1. Never ever make an enemy. No matter where you go to, they will pop up in an area where they have influence and you can least afford it.
2. Your reputation is everything—it's the one asset that no one can take away from you.
3. If you accept that life is about a balance of gaining wealth and giving back, you will always stay enriched.
4. If you are no longer learning and growing, retire to the beach.
5. If you can't say what you mean in two sentences, find a new vocabulary.
6. If you are not having fun, there is a problem.
7. Pack as much into a day as possible.

# WORDS OF WISDOM

BY MICHAEL JORDAAN

*Michael Jordaan is the former CEO of First National Bank.*

1. We are all suckers for recognition. Recognize and reward innovators.
2. Stuff the strong, only the innovative shall survive.
3. No one is as smart as everyone.
4. Take risks, make mistakes.

# LESSONS LEARNED IN MY FIRST EIGHTY YEARS

BY BYRON WIEN

*Byron Wien is an American investor and vice*

I was scheduled to speak about the world outlook at an investment conference recently and shortly before my time slot the conference organizer said the audience was more interested in what I had learned over the course of my career than what I had to say about the market. I jotted a few notes down and later expanded and edited what I said that day. I have since been encouraged to share my thoughts with a broader audience.

Here are some of the lessons I have learned in my first eighty years. I hope to continue to practice them in the next eighty.

1.  Concentrate on finding a big idea that will make an impact on the people you want to influence. The Ten Surprises, which I started doing in 1986, has been a defining product. People all over the world are aware of it and identify me with it. What they seem to like about it is that I put myself at risk by going on record with these events which I believe are probable and hold myself accountable at year-end. If you want to be successful and live a long, stimulating life, keep yourself at risk intellectually all the time.

2.  Network intensely. Luck plays a big role in life, and there is no better way to increase your luck than by knowing as many people as possible. Nurture your network. Write op-eds and thought pieces for major publications. Organize discussion groups to bring your thoughtful friends together.

3.  When you meet someone new, treat that person as a friend. Assume he or she is a winner and will become a positive force in your life. Most people wait for others to prove their value. Give them the benefit of the doubt from the start. Occasionally you will be disappointed, but your network will broaden rapidly if you follow this path.

4.  Read all the time. Don't just do it because you're curious about something, read actively. Have a point of view before you start a book or article and see if what you think is confirmed or

refuted by the author. If you do that, you will read faster and comprehend more.

5. Get enough sleep. Seven hours will do until you're sixty, eight from sixty to seventy, nine thereafter, which might include eight hours at night and a one-hour afternoon nap.

6. Evolve. Try to think of your life in phases so you can avoid a burnout. Do the number crunching in the early phase of your career. Try developing concepts later on. Stay at risk throughout the process.

7. Travel extensively. Try to get everywhere before you wear out. Attempt to meet local interesting people where you travel and keep in contact with them throughout your life. See them when you return to a place.

8. When meeting someone new, try to find out what formative experience occurred in their lives before they were seventeen. It is my belief that some important event in everyone's youth has an influence on everything that occurs afterward.

9. On philanthropy, my approach is to try to relieve pain rather than spread joy. Music, theatre, and art museums have many affluent supporters, give the best parties, and can add to your social lustre in a community. They don't need you. Social service, hospitals, and educational institutions can make the world a better place and help the disadvantaged make their way toward where they strive to be in life.

10. Younger people are naturally insecure and tend to overplay their accomplishments. Most people don't become comfortable with who they are until they're in their forties. By that time, they can underplay their achievements and become a nicer, more likeable person. Try to get to that point as soon as you can.

11. Take the time to give those who work for you a pat on the back when they do good work. Most people are so focused

on the next challenge that they fail to thank the people who support them. It is important to do this. It motivates and inspires people and encourages them to perform at a higher level.

12. When someone extends a kindness to you, write them a handwritten note, not an e-mail. Handwritten notes make an impact and are not quickly forgotten.

13. At the beginning of every year, think of ways you can do your job better than you have ever done it before. Write them down and look at what you have set out for yourself when the year is over.

14. The hard way is always the right way. Never take shortcuts, except when driving home from the Hamptons. Shortcuts can be construed as sloppiness, a career killer.

15. Don't try to be better than your competitors, try to be different. There is always going to be someone smarter than you, but there may not be someone who is more imaginative.

16. When seeking a career as you come out of school or making a job change, always take the job that looks like it will be the most enjoyable. If it pays the most, you're lucky. If it doesn't, take it anyway, I took a severe pay cut to take each of the two best jobs I've ever had, and they both turned out to be exceptionally rewarding financially.

17. There is a perfect job out there for everyone. Most people never find it. Keep looking. The goal of life is to be a happy person and the right job is essential to that.

18. When your children are grown or if you have no children, always find someone younger to mentor. It is very satisfying to help someone steer through life's obstacles, and you'll be surprised at how much you will learn in the process.

19. Every year try doing something you have never done before that is totally out of your comfort zone. It could be running a

marathon, attending a conference that interests you on an off-beat subject that will be populated by people very different from your usual circle of associates and friends, or travelling to an obscure destination alone. This will add to the essential process of self-discovery.

20. Never retire. If you work forever, you can live forever. I know there is an abundance of biological evidence against this theory, but I'm going with it anyway.

# "EXCELLENCE,"

BY LEWIS PUGH

*Lewis Pugh is an ocean advocate and a pioneer swimmer. In 2013, he was appointed Patron of the Oceans by the United Nations.*

The quickest way to get a job done is to do it with excellence the first time.

A few days into our journey to the North Pole, I was reminded of the lengths to which some people will go in the pursuit of excellence.

One of the members of our team was cameraman Chris Lotz. Chris's brief was, among other things, to capture images of polar bears.

Why polar bears? My North Pole swim was intended to highlight the melting of the Arctic sea ice, and the first casualties of the melting ice are polar bears, who need the ice in order to hunt for seals. Without sea ice, the polar bears will not survive. I knew that a strong image of a polar bear would communicate why I was doing this symbolic swim more than words ever could.

Now, you are not guaranteed to see a polar bear on the way to the North Pole. It takes seven days to get there and seven days back again. And since the first two days and the last two days are through open sea, you've effectively got just ten days in which to spot one.

Polar bears are white, and everything around you, all the way to the horizon, is white, so if you pass one on the ship, you might not even see it.

At the end of the second day, around dinnertime, I pulled Chris aside and reminded him about the polar bear images. The next day, when I came in to breakfast, Chris wasn't there. He wasn't there again for lunch, but I didn't think anything of it because there were two sittings for each meal. But when he still wasn't there at dinner, I thought, hold on, where's Chris?

I went down to his cabin—empty. I thought he might be filming on the upper deck, but he wasn't there. I checked in the cabin of a friend he used to visit—no luck. Twenty-four hours had now passed, and I started panicking. Had he fallen overboard?

I ran back to the upper deck of the ship again and this time, I looked properly, craning my head upward to take in the upper mast. And there I spotted Chris huddled behind the mast with the camera in his hand. I sprinted up two ladders to get to him, and asked him what he was doing.

"Lewis," he said, "inside the ship it's about 25°C. Outside, it's at least minus 25°C. If I take this camera from inside the ship straight to the outside, that's a drop of 50°C, and it will mist up and possibly even break." He'd been keeping the camera outside, wrapped in a protective tarpaulin, ready to go at a minute's notice. But that still didn't explain the missed meals. "What if a polar bear was sighted while I was inside?" Chris said. "It would take me precious minutes to get all my cold-weather gear on before I could come outside. I couldn't risk it. You asked me to get these pictures of a polar bear and that's what I'm doing."

Minutes later, a pair of polar bears walked in front of the ship—a mother and her cub. They jumped off the ice and swam across a patch of sea. Then the mother climbed out, with the cub not far behind her. It sprinted along after her as she disappeared into the horizon.

The entire scene took twenty-five minutes at most, and Chris got the whole thing, beginning to end.

Here's the rub: We never saw another polar bear for the rest of the expedition.

That's what I understand by the pursuit of excellence. Aristotle liked to say: "Excellence is not an act, but a habit." And former US Secretary of State Colin Powell said, "To achieve excellence in the big things, you have to develop the habit in little matters."

If you want to do a good job, the quickest and most effective way is with excellence. Because if you don't, you're going to have to go and do it again.

And you don't always get that second chance.

# LEADERSHIP MATTERS

BY BRAND PRETORIUS

*Brand Pretorius is the former CEO of McCarthy Motors.*

Leadership really matters. Put differently, everything rises and falls on leadership. It is the key enabler. In the tough world of business, it represents the organization's most potent competitive advantage. It is the source of every great achievement. The quality of self-leadership is the bedrock of every extraordinary life.

In my opinion, leadership has nothing to do with position, power or authority. It is all about influence, which has to be earned. In terms of the new paradigm of leadership, influence comes from something a lot deeper than positional power. It comes from the power of your ideals, the strength of your spirit, your humanity, and your ability to capture the hearts and minds of your people by caring about them, and by serving them. Before you can ask for a hand, you need to touch a heart.

The acid test for leaders is to live according to the right principles and values. And then to deliver the results. As leaders we therefore need to be hard headed when it comes to results, but to have gentle hearts when it comes to people.

In conclusion, our key task is to earn the trust, respect and confidence of each and every one of our team members by providing direction, by setting the right example at all times, and by achieving outstanding results.

# MANAGEMENT TIPS

by Alex Ferguson

*Alex Ferguson is the former manager of Manchester United.*

1. The job of a manager, like that of a teacher, is to inspire people to be better.

2. Give your team better technical skills, make them winners, make them better people, and they can go anywhere in life. When you give young people a chance, you not only create a longer life span for the team, you also create loyalty. They will always remember that you were the manager who gave them their first opportunity. Once they know you are batting for them, they will accept your way. You're fostering a sense of family. If you give young people your attention and an opportunity to succeed, it is amazing how much they will surprise you.

3. Never slack. Never allow a bad training session. What you see in training manifests itself on the game field. Never permit a lack of focus. It's about constant intensity, concentration, and speed. That's what makes players improve with each session.

4. Lift players' expectations. They should never give in. "If you give in once, you'll give in twice."

5. Never lose control. Especially when you are dealing with thirty top professionals who are all millionaires. If any players want to take you on, to challenge your authority and control, deal with them. There are occasions when you have to ask yourself whether certain players are affecting the dressing-room atmosphere, the performance of the team, and your control of the players and staff. If they are, you have to cut the cord. There is absolutely no other way. It doesn't matter if the person is the best player in the world.

6. Many people do not fully understand the value of observing. Observation is a critical part of management.

7. Manage change. Most people with a successful track record don't look to change. The greatest leaders know they couldn't afford not to change. Work hard. Treat every success as your first. Your job is to give your team the best possible chance of winning.

# TRUE TALES OF A FUN, FEARLESS FEMALE

BY JANE RAPHAELY

*Jane Raphaely is the founder of Associated Magazines.*

Jane grew up in a poor household in war-torn England. She was able to escape poverty, get an education, travel the world, find love, start a family, and build some of South Africa's most successful and influential women's magazines.

These are some of the lessons learned from her book:

## 1. Work Hard

Growing up in a poor community in Stockport, England, during the Second World War, Jane used her mother's name to become an agent for a mail-order company. On weekends, she worked at a shoe shop, and at night, she babysat.

She describes the "game" of trying to do as much as she could as "not so much a case of beating the system, but more like beating the clock. Time was the enemy."

## 2. Take Risks and Seize Opportunities

Working hard is not always enough. You need to take risks. Jane demonstrated this by taking part in a Name That Tune game show in the middle of her studies. She also took on a massive risk when she started Fair Lady, Cosmopolitan, and

O magazines in South Africa.

## 3. Always Start a Venture with a Party

The launch parties for Cosmopolitan and O were huge and extravagant, and they set the scene and tone for both magazines in South Africa. They created awareness and showcased the brands.

## 4. Have a Charming Sales Team

Jane never interviewed the writers; she believed that she could tell everything she needed from the words on a page. She did, however, interview anyone who would come into contact with advertisers and the public. Advertising is the lifeblood of any magazine, and these people needed to charm, be liked, and impress.

## 5. Face Your Fears

Jane describes how she overcame her intense fear of public speaking while on the Name That Tune game show. Her ability to speak in public helped her earn money as a student and became a factor in her success as an editor and businesswoman.

## 6. Don't Back Down from Confrontation

Throughout most of her time as editor of Fair Lady and Cosmopolitan, Jane had to appeal against the censorship board for the right to publish articles. These appeals created publicity for the magazines and improved their readership.

Once she managed to get the rights to publish Cosmopolitan magazine, she discovered that Caxton Publishers had already registered the name in South Africa. She was forced to face Caxton for the name rights.

She didn't back down. She fought.

## 7. Be Confident in Your Abilities

Jane built up a magazine empire by presenting confidence to her readers, who often wanted to be like her, and to her financial backers, who took comfort from her confidence to create and manage successful magazines.

**NOTE TO SELF**

Learn to receive help!

# "NOTES TO SELF,"

BY KIM VAN KETS

*Kim van Kets is the author of Tri the Beloved Country,*
*the story of how she ran, swam, and cycled the circumference of*
*South Africa.*

1. Focus on the Good Stuff!

> *Find a place inside where there is joy,*
> *and the joy will burn out the pain.*
>
> — JOSEPH CAMPBELL —

2. Find out what makes you come alive (what makes your heart beat hardest) and don't ever give it up! Never. Not for anything.

> *Each of us has a fire in our hearts for something.*
> *It's our goal in life to find it and keep it lit.*
>
> — MARY LOU RETTON —

3. Achieving your unique dream is within your grasp. It is not something reserved for the chosen few.

4. Translate your dream into a goal.

> *A dream is just a dream.*
> *A goal is a dream with a plan and a deadline.*
>
> — HARVEY MACKAY —

5. Self-discipline/routine holds things together in the tough times.

6. Ingrain discipline and routine in the good times, because

when the bad times come, it is only the routine that keeps things together. As Winston Churchill put it, "When you are going through hell, keep going!"

7. Reward yourself—but only when you deserve it.

8. In this age of instant gratification, don't forget the incredible motivational power of deprivation and reward.

9. Learn to ask for and accept help.

10. Get out of your comfort zone.

11. Being comfortable is both necessary and nice, but it cannot be sustained indefinitely. Force yourself out of complacency in order to develop and grow.

12. When the resources you have always relied upon dry up, get creative.

13. When your budgets/gadgets/energy/water disappear, there is always a solution. Stay calm and creatively seek it. The earth has boundless potential and so do you.

14. Expect and plan for the difficulty of change. Even good change is tricky.

15. Take time to take care of the important stuff before you find a crisis on your hands. Preventative maintenance is key. This is equally true of health, financial, and relationship issues.

16. Don't let the enormity of your challenge immobilize you. Keep moving.

*Nobody trips over mountains.*
*It is the stones in your path that cause you to stumble.*
*Navigate your way across the stones,*
*and you will find you have crossed the mountain.*

— UNKNOWN —

17. Your body is an awesome machine. It is for this reason that you must love, respect, and admire it.

18. Your body's value lies in its ability to master its environment. Treat it as a machine, not an ornament.

19. Listen to your heart.

20. Do not listen to the prophet of doom (even when it's you). Keep calm and proceed with that thing that you are compelled to do.

21. Have fun! Especially as a team/family. It will give you energy.

22. Surround yourself with the right team. Find people who share your passion, make you laugh, and have the same sense of the bizarre.

23. Learn to say, "I am so sorry, I totally screwed up. I will fix this." Proviso: You should never apologize for something that you are not responsible for.

# HOW TO ACHIEVE SUCCESS

BY YUSUF ABRAMJEE

*Yusuf Abramjee is founder of Lead SA and Crime Line.*

Passion, commitment, and dedication are critical factors. If you wake up in the morning and you find no joy going to work, go and find another job. Do what you love most. Do it from the heart and you will succeed.

Remember the basic international leadership principles and work toward them: "Model the way; inspire a shared vision; challenge the process; enable others to act; and encourage the heart."

Doing good is important. We must never forget to help others in need. Charity must always be top of mind. We all aspire to become wealthy—but never forget those in need.

Ask yourself everyday what legacy you want to leave.

Become an active citizen. Stand up for what's right and make a difference; remember these tips and you will find success.

# LETTER FROM A DAD

Dear Son,

Don't ever waste a single second of your life.

You are young, invincible. Never conceive of your life coming to an end. But it will, and as you grow older, it will pass you by at an ever-increasing speed.

And there is nothing worse than trying to cram in lost years as you feel you are running out of time.

Make sure you have fun in whatever you do. And remember hard work can be real fun too.

Don't forget to fall in love, out of love, and back in love when you are young. It's much easier and less painful than when you are old.

Life is tough, and you will have to be tough to get through it. Don't confuse being tough with being cruel to anyone or anything. Tough just means hanging on to everything that means so much to you when the world is trying to rip it apart. And if you make it, the world will not love you for being successful. But don't let that ever make you settle for average or mediocre.

Be the most you ever can be, and you will have no regrets.

Be kind whenever you can, as long as it never compromises your principles and values. Every kindness you show will make you a happier man.

And if you should ever have power, be careful how you use it. Wield it only to make the world a better place. Never to make you feel better about yourself.

Be humble in success and brave in failure. And there will be more failures than successes. So suck back your tears early on in life. Let them only flow when you are bursting, since they have a habit of draining the energy you so desperately need just to survive.

Don't ever lie, except if it is a clear kindness to someone who needs a touch of kindness.

Read and read and read.

Laugh whenever you can. It will energize you and those around you.

Always build. Anything. Anywhere. Try and leave something you can look back upon and be proud of, something you can touch.

Have the courage to be decisive. It will make you move more quickly. Be sure of yourself, but not so sure that you cannot learn from anyone. Be confident, but never be brash.

Don't be loud.

Be gentle. Be respectful. Be generous.

Look everyone in the eye. And never blink!

Smile when your heart tells you to. That's how you touch people's hearts.

And remember, in the end, everything always works out okay.

Love,

Dad

## LESSONS FROM WINSTON CHURCHILL

*Winston Churchill was prime minister of Britain
during World War II.*

1. There is no time for ease and comfort. It is time to dare and endure.

2. In war, resolution; in defeat, defiance; in victory, magnanimity.

3. If you are going through hell, keep going.

4. It is no use saying, "We are doing our best." You must succeed in doing what is necessary.

5. An appeaser is one who feeds a crocodile—hoping it will eat him last.

6. Never give in—never, never, never, never—in nothing great or small, large or petty, never give in except to convictions of honor and good sense. Never yield to force; never yield to the apparently overwhelming might of the enemy.

7. If you will not fight for right when you can easily win without bloodshed, if you will not fight when your victory is sure and not too costly, you may come to the moment when you will have to fight with all the odds against you and only a precarious chance of survival. There may even be a worse case. You may have to fight when there is no hope of victory, because it is better to perish than to live as slaves.

8. Men occasionally stumble over the truth, but most of them pick themselves up and hurry off as if nothing has happened.

9. You have enemies? Good. That means you've stood up for something, sometime in your life.

10. Some see private enterprise as a predatory target to be shot, others as a cow to be milked, but few are those who see it as a sturdy horse pulling the wagon.

11. Socialists think profits are a vice; I consider losses the real vice.

12. Character may be manifested in the great moments, but it is made in the small ones.

13. If you have an important point to make, don't try to be subtle or clever. Use a pile driver. Hit the point once. Then come back and hit it again. Then hit it a third time—a tremendous whack.

14. When you have to kill a man, it costs nothing to be polite.

15. Nothing in life is so exhilarating as to be shot at without result.

16. To improve is to change; to be perfect is to change often.

17. Success is not final; failure is not fatal: it is the courage to continue that counts.

## TEN WAYS TO CHANGE THE WORLD

by Admiral William McRaven

*Admiral William H. McRaven shares lessons learnt in basic SEAL training.*

1. Make your bed in the morning. Start the day with a task done. The sense of achievement will give you momentum for other jobs.

2. To get through the waves, everyone must paddle together. Teamwork wins wars.

3. Measure a person by the size of his heart, not the size of his feet.

4. Sometimes no matter how hard you prepare, you end up as a sugar cookie (wet, cold, and covered in sand). Failure happens. Get over it, keep moving forward.

5. You will fail. You will likely fail often. It will be painful. It will be discouraging. At times it will test you to your very core. (See point 4.)

6. If you want to win sometimes you have to charge into the obstacle headfirst. Go flat out.

7. Don't back down from the sharks. If you're going to be taken down, go down fighting.

8. You must be your very best in the darkest moment.

9. Start singing when you're up to your neck in mud. It will give your team an extra boost.

10. Never, ever ring the bell. Never give up. Keep fighting.

# DANGERS TO HUMAN VIRTUE

BY MAHATMA GANDHI

*The Mahatma liberated India from British colonial rule.*

1. Wealth without work
2. Business without ethics
3. Politics without principle
4. Religion without sacrifice
5. Science without humanity
6. Pleasure without conscience
7. Knowledge without character

# "TEN TIPS FROM A BUDDHIST MONK"

*Charlene Barry is founder of This Is Project Me.*

Is there any doubt that people are searching for happiness in the wrong places?

Reaching a fulfilled lifestyle is much more than just a beautiful home or modern car. It's about connecting with yourself on more than just a conscious level.

Buddhist monks have figured this out. Instead of chasing material value, they look within.

The following tips come from monks who know what a fulfilled life entails.

## 1. Never Stop Trying

The worst thing technology has taught us is to be lazy.

According to a monk, it is crucial to try several times before giving up. It is also important to try different approaches. When you have reached the point where nothing works, then make peace and move on, but giving up after only trying once leads to a life of disappointment.

Creating any practice or new habit requires patience and a "never-stop-trying" attitude.

## 2. All the Answers Come from Within

A fundamental principle for monks is to use intuition.

In order to deal with problems the world throws at you, you need to use your sixth sense. Buddhism students are only given a small amount of information from which they have to solve big problems. This is part of their preparation for facing the world.

In essence the universe will open the door, but you need to

walk through it without losing sight or becoming disappointed when the answer isn't clear from the start is a discipline we must try to master.

All the answers reside within us; we just need to look in the right places and trust ourselves.

### 3. Failure Equals Growth

This is a lesson very few people seem to understand. Making a mistake or failing at something tends to make us focus on the worst.

Keep in mind that there are always two sides to a coin. Failures and mistakes are a learning process and a precious one at that. Someone can teach you a valuable lesson, but unless you actually go through it yourself, it won't hold as much value.

Taking chances is such a critical part of a fulfilled life, yet we are scared to take part in the learning process.

Monks know there are two sides to everything in life: with good must come bad, just like with growth must come failure, and a lot of this comes down to one's perspective.

### 4. Know the Power of Impermanence

Impermanence is one of the most important Buddhist teachings, and one that must be fully understood and accepted in order to fully understand life.

Nothing is permanent, and the sooner you understand what this really means and accept this, you will be able to live a life filled with less expectation from anything and anyone.

The only thing that is constant is change itself, and when you can learn to embrace change, beautiful things begin to shift in our lives.

### 5. Learn the Art of Patience

For some people, patience is the hardest thing to achieve.

Notice how these people become angry and agitated quite quickly?

There is a time and place for everything. Time is man-made and should never cause you frustration. Patience is a true virtue. When you are capable of controlling it, you are well on your way to living a more fulfilled life.

### 6. Forget about What Other People Think

Society has a way of programming our egos. We are constantly aware of what other people might be thinking or saying about us.

Feeding the ego is by no means healthy, and even though we think it results in happiness, we are greatly mistaken. Keeping your ego happy doesn't mean that you are happy.

The monks suggest that you detach from your ego, this is what will allow you to grow spiritually.

You need to focus on your own thoughts rather than the thoughts of those around you. Be in tune with yourself, not others.

### 7. Fight the Enemy Within

You might think your biggest enemy is your boss or the bully at school, but it's not. You are the one who gives power to your fears and insecurities.

Before you can accomplish anything, you need to tackle the enemy that empowers the elements keeping you from happiness. In other words, overcome your internal fears.

### 8. Happiness Starts from Within

It will be I to assume that happiness is only based on the spiritual side of life.

Family, friends, music, books, and hobbies all form part of your journey. However, you cannot enjoy anything if you are not happy internally.

Once you reach happiness from within, it will manifest outside in the people and things that make life worth living.

Meditation is such a significant practice for monks because it helps to cultivate peace from the inside out, and when you become more in touch with your true self, the happier you will feel.

## 9. Be Present

We hear this one all the time but really, you should stop and think about how present you are right in this moment.

Monks are so aware of being present in this moment as it is the only moment they can be sure of.

If we learn to do our best, act our best, feel our best, and just be for this moment only, then we will be able to live a much more fulfilled, quality life.

Meditation is invaluable for anyone who is finding it difficult to practice staying present.

## 10. Know What Is More Valuable than Material Possessions

Living in a world dominated by media influences, it can be difficult to not get drawn toward material things.

To shield yourself, create a grounding board. Fill this board with pictures of people less fortunate than yourself, children who have no food or clean water, animals that are being treated poorly, a picture of your grandparents, family, your favorite yoga balance, words that express feelings like love, compassion, family, friends—things that mean a lot to you.

Looking at a picture of your grounding board will help to pull you back to what is really important in life.

# BOOKS TO READ

*Outside of a dog, a book is man's best friend.*
*Inside of a dog, it's too dark to read.*

— GROUCHO MARX —

## ANTIFRAGILE, *by Nassim Taleb*

Taleb's basic premise is that we can find ourselves in one of three states:

- Fragile (you are exposed to adversity, a big, negative effect)
- Resilient (you are shielded from adversity, and there is no effect)
- Antifragile (you gain from adversity, a big, positive effect)

These states can be applied to your health, finances, and emotional well-being.

**Other takeaways:**

1. Beware "touristification," the tendency of a tourist to stick to a fixed agenda rather than to go with the flow. Taleb argues that you should start the journey and see what happens from there. It's difficult following a life filled with uncertainty, but it's a far richer way of living.

2. The path to your destiny is not identifying what you love. Rather it's via negativa, something that eliminates what you don't love. By using the via negativa thought process, you systematically eliminate the people and things you don't enjoy until you're left with your core. That's how you find happiness.

3. Someone once asked Michelangelo how he carved the statue David. His reply, "Easy. I started with a block of marble and chipped away everything that was not David."

4. Many people (especially academics) believe that their teachings result in the success of students. They create a backward narrative that justifies their work. Taleb argues that most teachers have no impact. It doesn't matter how much you lecture baby birds on how to fly, they're going to fly anyway.

5. Economic development leads to education, not the other way around.

6. Doers are more important than thinkers.

7. If you need more than one reason, you're lying. The French army would discipline soldiers if they had more than one reason for absenteeism.

8. Never buy anything advertised. If it has to be advertised, it's not the best.

9. Don't use doctors. The incentives to overmedicate are too strong. The medical profession should only be resorted to in times of dire emergency.

Taleb's conclusion is that life is about taking risks, and taking risks is about having courage. If you take risks and you face your fate with dignity, there is nothing you can do that is not small. If you do not take risks, there is nothing you can do that will make you grand. The ultimate antifragility is fearlessness. If you can overcome fear, you can take over the world.


## THE HARD THING ABOUT HARD THINGS,
*by Ben Horowitz*

1. When raising money, look for a market of one. When you only need one investor to say yes, so it's best to ignore the other thirty who say no.

2. If you're going to eat shit, don't nibble. Give bad news or take pain all in one go rather than drag it out over months.

3. Figuring out the right product is the innovator's job, not the customer's job. Innovators need a combination of knowledge, skill, and courage to ignore the data and give the customer what he didn't know he wanted.

4. Start-up CEOs should not play the odds. You have no choice but to find the answer, so don't hedge yourself.

5. Product is king. If you're being beaten on product, you need

to knuckle down and fix it, rather than sell harder or redesign the organogram. There are no silver bullets for fixing bad product, only lead bullets.

6. Managing by numbers is like painting by numbers. Strictly for amateurs.

7. Lazy people decisions result in "management debt." For example: Two-in-a-box (comanagers), overcompensating an employee, or no performance review system. Management debt is always repaid, with interest. Avoid at all costs.

## THE OBSTACLE IS THE WAY, *by Ryan Holliday*

Ryan Holliday's book is a super-entertaining introduction to stoicism, filled with a plethora of mental tools for dealing with adversity and setbacks. In other words, it's a perfect manual for aspiring heroes.

What else is life if not dealing with adversity and obstacles? Taking risks means sometimes things won't go your way. That's where your mind-set is the difference between survival and failure.

**Some tips for the right mind-set:**

1. Accept that bad stuff happens. Keep trying your best.

2. You get what you want by letting it go.

3. This is it. The game is on now.

4. Things are what they are.

5. No one will save you.

6. The only hero is you.

7. This too shall pass.

Ryan's book will help you get your head right. If you're trying to get ahead in your life, personally or professionally, you need to find the way past obstacles. This book will show you how to turn the obstacle in to the way.

**Books on STOIC PHILOSOPHY:**

**Courage under Fire,** *by James Stockdale*

**Stoicism and the Art of Happiness,** *by Donald Robertson*

**Meditations: A New Translation,** *by Marcus Aurelius and Gregory Hays*

**Seven Secrets to Being a Multi-Millionaire,** *by Lewis Schiff*

**Extract from BUSINESS BRILLIANT**

1. Follow your passion and then follow the money. The money will not follow you.

2. Play to your strengths. Delegate your weaknesses.

3. It's all about your network.

4. Heads I win, tails I don't lose. No need to risk your personal savings. Make sure you've protected your downside and then chase upside.

5. Copy rather than invent. Fast followers make more money than first movers.

6. Save less. To get rich, you need to earn more.

7. Avoid debt at all costs.

**IF YOU MEET THE BUDDHA**
**ON THE ROAD, KILL HIM,** *by Sheldon Kopp*

1. Never stop moving.

2. We are all just struggling human beings.

3. "You cannot cheat an honest man." T. S. Eliot

4. There is no teacher. You are responsible for your own growth.

5. We have one life. We can choose any path, so choose the path of the heart.

6. Walk into the lion's den. The most important things, each man

must do for himself.

7. Don't feel sympathy for others. There is no master and slave. Victims feed off sympathy.

**The essence of Kopp's book is this:**

Stop waiting for salvation. No one will save you. Only you can save you. Take responsibility for your life.

## OTHER BOOKS TO READ:

- Seeking Wisdom, *by Peter Bevelin*
- Guns, Germs, and Steel, *by Jared Diamond*
- Uncertainty, *by Jonathan Fields*
- Selling the Invisible, *by Harry Beckwith*
- The Righteous Mind, *by Jonathan Haidt*
- Cyrus the Great, *by Larry Hedrick*
- The Outsiders, *by William Thorndike*

*Share your knowledge.*
*It's a way to achieve immortality.*

— THE DALAI LAMA —

DON'T FORCE YOUR MISSION DOWN PEOPLE'S THROATS

JOSEPH CAMPBELL

# 13

## THE END

# LUCK IS REAL

*Luck is a dividend of sweat.*
*The more you sweat, the luckier you get.*

— Ray Kroc —

No one is entirely self-made; everyone had some luck along the way.

Having said that, true entrepreneurs never say "luck is everything." That's a fatalistic way of looking at the world. Worse, it can be a crutch for excusing why you're not successful. When you read the stories of great men and women, they all say the same thing: "Luck is where opportunity meets preparation."

Some people spend their whole lives preparing for and never coming across opportunity. That's bad luck, and that's why you should do what you love. At least then if the dice don't fall in your favor, you won't have wasted your life.

Accept that luck plays a big role in your life, and then put your head down and work.

Success is 90 percent luck and 10 percent hard work. Don't try it without the 10 percent.

*Remember that not getting what you want*
*is sometimes a wonderful stroke of luck.*

— THE DALAI LAMA —

# BELIEVE IN YOURSELF

*To believe in the things you can*
*see and touch is no belief at all;*
*but to believe in the unseen*
*is a triumph and a blessing.*

— ABRAHAM LINCOLN —

Life is unpredictable. The only time you know how something will turn out is before you start.

**Step One:**

Get comfortable with uncertainty.

**Step Two:**

Manage your reactions to adversity and obstacles. Getting upset and blaming the world will get you nowhere. When you hit a roadblock, keep calm and get creative.

**Step Three:**

Close your eyes and learn how to trust.

There will come a time in your journey when you simply cannot see the way forward. You just can't be sure you'll make it. The worst mistake you'll make is to freeze; therein lies guaranteed failure. At the same time, you'll know you're so far in that there's no going back. The only way is straight ahead. Keep moving forward.

Trust that everything will be okay and believe in yourself.

# THE SECRET TO ACHIEVING YOUR DREAMS

Ignore all steps between you and your final destination, except the next step. Take that step. Look up and make sure you're still on track for the goal, and then look down and take the next step. Repeat until you reach the destination.

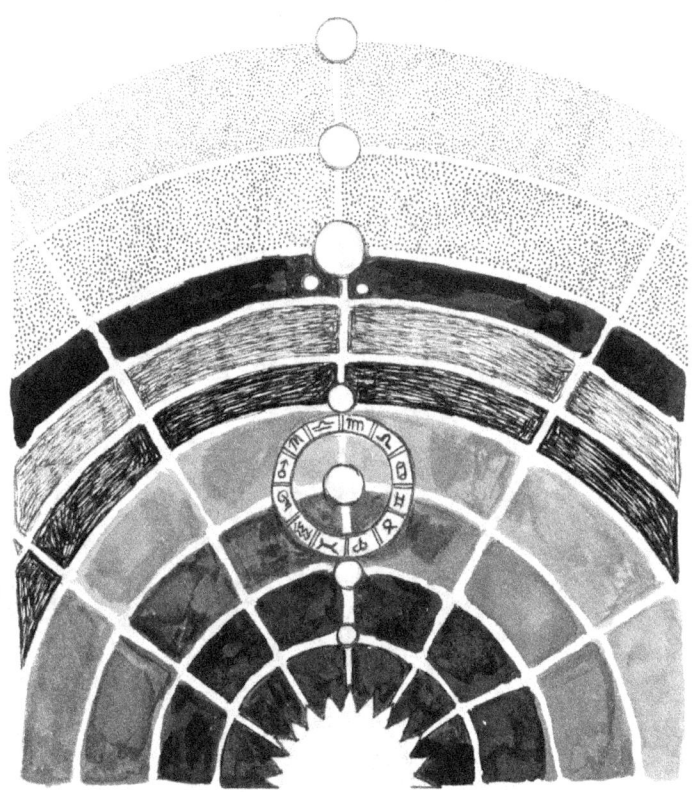

*It's a mistake to look too far ahead.*
*Only one link in the chain of destiny*
*can be handled at a time.*

— Winston Churchill —

# ABOUT THE AUTHOR
## Alan Knott-Craig

Alan Knott-Craig is a successful entrepreneur, best-selling author, and founder of Project Isizwe, an NGO rolling out free Wi-Fi in poor communities across Africa.

Originally from Pretoria, he studied at Nelson Mandela Metropolitan University (formerly UPE). He qualified as a chartered accountant in 2002 and has subsequently invested in or funded twenty-seven companies in the telecoms, media, and tech industry.

Alan was named as a Young Global Leader by the World Economic Forum in 2009. Forbes listed him as one of the top-ten young African millionaires to watch. He was also included in "100 Choiseul Africa," a list of top one hundred young African business leaders in 2014, 2015, and 2016. He was nominated as the 2015 ICT Personality of the Year by ITWeb.

Alan has a passion for entrepreneurship and a dream that all Africans will one day have free Wi-Fi.

www.bigalmanack.com

DESIGN & LAYOUT
Carel de Beer

COVER PHOTOS
storyblocks.com

ILLUSTRATION
Carel de Beer, Marli Fourie & Mia du Plessis

www.ingramcontent.com/pod-product-compliance
Lightning Source LLC
Chambersburg PA
CBHW051310220526
45468CB00004B/1285